French Flair

Sébastien Siraudeau

French Flair

Flammarion

Contents

Decorating is an art of living, a way of cultivating your surroundings in order to feel comfortable—whether cocooning or entertaining, relaxing or receiving guests. French design is all about juxtaposing unexpected and unconventional combinations to create a unique home. Any style can be adapted to a house in the city or the country, to an apartment or a château; it just calls for imagination and an approach free of preconceived notions. Anything is possible, it's a frame of mind—it's inspiration via decoration.

From traditional to eclectic, or from contemporary to natural, this volume demonstrates that the possibilities are endless. Discover the rustic, rugged, and homely feel of the residences unveiled in a chapter devoted to authentic interiors. Enjoy daydreaming in idyllic, romantic atmospheres, surrounded by flowing fabrics and whimsical touches. Create an eclectic living space full of bold colors and prints, juxtaposed with unusual objects. Or reproduce grand, sophisticated, and elegant interiors reminiscent of a French château, complete with crimson velvet and fine upholstery. Through the exploration of seven different yet complementary styles, a profusion of ideas is revealed to add a certain French flair to your home.

The 111 locations featured in this book are the product of four years of travels throughout France; four years of discoveries, encounters, and exchanges. Let yourself be guided through the extraordinary destinations replete with French panache and inspiration that are compiled in this extensive work, from rural guesthouses to charming antique shops to seaside retreats; enjoy them from the comforts of your own home, or use the address book to plot your course to visit these rare and exceptional places in person. Happy travels!

Authentic

The school of life

LA FONTAINE DE GRÉGOIRE
Guesthouse

The setting is rustic, the owner gruff—a "real character," you might think, on a first meeting. A product of the Aubrac mountain air, the reclusive life here in Saint-Urcize? He has a *buron* (a traditional shepherd's hut for making cheese) and a Citroën Mehari jeep. He's also the owner of a local institution, Chez Remise—a hotel, restaurant, bar, tobacco store, and newspaper stand run with his wife Isabelle, and family. The voluble band of local anglers have made it their headquarters. Fred Remise—for that is his name—knows every nook of the local river and mountain. Everyone knows him, too. And suddenly Saint-Urcize seems like the center of the world. Thanks to Fred, people came here first to fish. There were stirrings of life at the hotel. Then Fred and Isabelle renovated the old village school, in order to have bigger bedrooms. They gave it the name of the fountain on the village square. Now Saint-Urcize is a place of pilgrimage—not least for dinner chez Bras, in nearby Laguiole. Why not carry on to Santiago de Compostela? The old pilgrims' route passes further down the mountain.

A cosy, scholarly retreat

Where's Fred? Saint-Urcize is a small place, and Fred is never far from his hotel in the village's old school.

Every morning, he's first up to light the fire in the great hearth, beside which stands "his" favorite armchair.

The table stands in the midst of a space resembling a colorful, jumbled traveler's notebook in three dimensions:

a cheerful accumulation of objects and vintage finds brought back from heaven knows where,

each telling its own story.

Large volumes, carved panels, opulent bathrooms, and hidden touches of fantasy. Fred and
Isabelle have already devoted nine years to transforming the old school building, which
is destined for new plans in future. For the moment, everything is happening in the garden:
Fred has commissioned a student landscape gardener—his "protégé"—to redesign it, carte blanche.
The approach is typical of his profoundly humanist, philanthropic outlook. With a keen eye, too,
for the mountain and its wildflowers, the crucible of his personal school of (bohemian) life.

In remembrance

LA BROCANTE DE JEANNE
Collectibles

In Brittany, the Char à Banc is a name known to all. This farm and adjacent mill was converted into an all-purpose inn in the 1970s and here the Lamour family busies itself serving unpretentious fare, airing guestrooms, and amusing children. Their taste for old things and their love of local heritage snowballed, and the premises have even housed an agricultural eco-museum with an old plow and tractors on their last wheels.

La Maison Bleue, nestled in the basement of the four-hundred-year-old granite mill, was the brainchild of Jeanne, the mom and now grandmother of this hardworking troop. A tireless hunter of vintage pieces, you don't need to be told that Jeanne has an insatiable appetite for old crockery. The *brocante* overflows with cabinets full of faience and tin utensils, but also with more rustic objects, from zinc pitchers to a cute statuette of the Virgin which in former times would have watched over hearth and home. Still, it would all be far less effective without the displays in red, green, blue, and yellow composed by one of her daughters, Céline, into a homey environment that encourages enthusiastic exploration.

Grandma's kitchen

Piles of plates and terrines, towers of ramekins and cups, batches of glasses,
dishcloths, and tea towels, enameled kettles and coffee jugs, drainers and strainers,
soup tureens, casseroles, and saucepans. La Maison Bleue deals in the most
delightful kitchenware. In this well-lit and (deliberately) chaotic bazaar,
once common objects begin to acquire the allure of a unique piece. Even if you come
across the odd crack, chip, or nick, it hardly matters as there are enough dishes here
to compose a week's worth of table settings and services. From pieces from the Digoin
et Sarreguemines workshop—with its floral or geometrical patterns that go so well
with the subtle blue of a Saint-Uze piece—to the cream-colored Gien collection,
or a cracked Charolles dish, the stock offers a tour of French crockery. And don't forget to
grab a jar of Char à Banc's homemade rhubarb jam on your way out.

Art and old stones

LA GRANDE MAISON, ARTEDU
Bed-and-breakfast,
restaurant, workshops

Bohemian tastes. The sound of an accordion is heard in the narrow lanes, lined with hollyhocks, of a village in the Auvergne. In this poetic moment, time stands still. Nihad is Bosnian. And an accordion player. He's rehearsing here, in the workshop at La Grande Maison, for a forthcoming concert in Amsterdam. The austere front facade of the building is impressive: five stories built in the fifteenth century, on the slopes of a rocky outcrop atop which stands the Romanesque abbey of Chanteuges. This seemingly raw setting has been brought back to life thanks to creative workshops run by Dutch painter Marloes der Kinderen. Steeped in the house's powerful atmosphere—it was once the home of a family of writers—Marloes has been careful to preserve its history. When she first moved in, the house was filled with objects, letters, and books, the source of her decorative inspiration.

A life-size canvas

Much of the furniture has never left the house. Marloes has also sourced pieces from around the region, and elsewhere in France, amassing myriad small collections in the process. Straw hats, terra-cotta pots, worn-out books, and dismembered picture frames are scattered throughout the house, like objects on a life-size canvas. On the floors, Marloes, an artist, has improvised graphic, engraved designs. The walls are hung with a multitude of small collages composed of fragments from the childhood writings of the house's former owner. Words and pictures that echo one another, linger and entice, like the accordion music fading gently in the narrow streets of Chanteuges, a place that's very hard to leave.

Trifling objects

LA BROCANTE DE LA BRUYÈRE
Collectibles

Picardy—from Survilliers to Amiens via Crèvecoeur-le-Grand or Abbeville—is no stranger to junk markets and *réderies*, as they call garage sales here. La Brocante de la Bruyère is planted in one of those red-brick farms so characteristic of the region's countryside. Although not far from the well-heeled cities of Chantilly and Senlis, one can still come across some great "steals" that make out-of-town *brocantes* so much fun. With a hearty nod in the direction of the famous racecourse nearby, our eye was initially caught by a stable of model horses.

Then, all higgledy-piggledy, one comes across an embroidered alphabet primer, a rusty Tolix-type stool, wooden toys, zinc vanes, and a weathercock. And this is just a tiny sample of the unfussy stock Florence has arranged in her gorgeous country farmstead.

The intimate *brocante*

FANETTE W.
Antiques and collectibles

From the banks of the Seine to the coast, Normandy's long
and winding roads are flanked by countless *brocantes*.
One just has to stop at Rouen, between the famous town
clock and its vertiginous cathedral. Here, Fanette W.,
daughter of an antique dealer from Lyon, energetically
pilots a going concern in curios, tradesmen's tools, and
smaller pieces of country furniture, located behind the
traditional half-timbered houses of the rue Eau-de-Robec.
The eye first alights on a strange totem studded with
nails, a big plaster nose, a birdcage, a draper's rule, a
worn chest of drawers, before flitting on to some wooden
statuettes. The collection of diverse portraits—hung as if
in some humanist's private gallery—gets Fanette talking,

and the unknown sitters gradually come into focus, such as "her" gypsy or "her" little gent, who, in spite of their reticent looks, turn heads. Among all the canvases, there are naturally some seascapes painted in oils, in which schooners and three-masters tell the story of the harbor of a hundred bell towers.

From the quayside, the Seine winds down to Honfleur and the seaside resorts of the now flourishing coast, where—from the enchanting La Vie à la Campagne, dedicated to every conceivable type of garden article, to the well-named boutique of Mise en Scène at Trouville—vintage and antique dealers are part of the landscape.

A converted boathouse

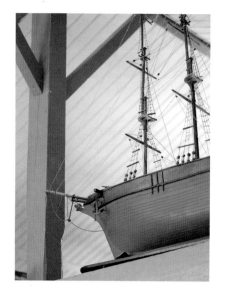

LE LOFT
Vacation apartment

A shaft of sunlight strikes the Eiffel Tower, and every Parisian's fancy turns to thoughts of escape. The sweeping waterscapes of the Somme estuary are the French capital's nearest (seaside) port of call: the beach at Crotoy, Marquenterre nature reserve, the harbor at Saint-Valery. Picardy's corner of seaside heaven is well-loved for its cobbled quaysides, authentic charm, and fabulous seafood market. The region's brick-and-timber fishermen's cottages are in high demand, and every metropolitan weekender dreams of finding a small, well-equipped hideaway for a breath of sea air. Would a stylish loft be too much to ask? Sophie and Patrick Deloison have created just that, in an old boathouse converted with flair and skill by Patrick himself, a beachcombing handyman and professional antiques dealer. The tall building is divided into two levels. The ground floor is a working antiques warehouse, while the loft occupies the "cathedral" mezzanine above—a wooden structure built by a ship's carpenter and decorated in imaginative, theatrical style, using found objects and cleverly recycled pieces put to new uses. The essence of seaside charm.

Scrubbed driftwood, bare brick, heavy
wooden floorboards, natural linen. Hanging
like fishermen's ex-votos from the rafters, a flotilla
of miniature canoes, junks, and other assorted
craft. The Robinson Crusoe interior is flooded
with natural light from ten glass doors ranged
along one wall, like a Parisian artist's studio.

A curious buffalo-head trophy above a painting
by Robert Hanès (a long-time resident of
Saint-Valery). Separating the bedroom from
the bathroom, an openwork balustrade
from a *café-dancing* in a nearby village.

TE

BROCANTE →

The ABCs of bargain-hunting

LA GARÇONNIÈRE
Private collection

This is one of the newest *brocantes* in the district. With a wink to the bevies of girls who staff the nearby stores, "the boys" opened their Garçonnière in fall 2006 having cut their teeth elsewhere. (A *garçonnière* is a "bachelor pad"—and this one is a secret den especially for male lovers of vintage.) Though here and there one spots an errant doll or an old feather fan, the pickings in this tiny hideaway are for the most part "masculine." Not exclusively of course, but it has to be admitted that the backlit SENLIS-PARIS sign and the 1970s advertising bills for Michelin ZX tires would be more at home in an apartment belonging to someone with a taste for mechanical gizmos. Still, in La Garçonnière these objects have to compete for space with old mirrors, display units and bar tables, a postman's bicycle, and wooden lockers.

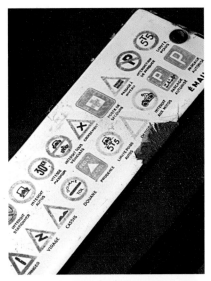

Lettering, markers, signposts

The *garçons* have a predilection for signposts and signs in general, for the road or elsewhere, and have amassed a collection of letters and numbers of every style: phone booth signs, parking space numbers, old zinc lettering, an elevator indicator, a board inscribed "Bois de Vincennes," a laminated highway code crib sheet. The game consists in guessing the period and then in discovering new uses or novel meanings: rearrange the letters into someone's name or, failing this, into your children's initials; invent weird and wonderful acronyms; pick out your house number, your date of birth, or an anniversary you should never forget. And all this fun with letters and graphics is, of course, most edifying.

Ocean bounty

LA BROCANTE D'OUESSANT
Collectibles

An antiques and bric-a-brac shop, on Ouessant island, France's westernmost outpost. Paul Townsend (known locally as l'Anglais, although his grandfather was a Ouessant fisherman) came ashore here twenty years ago in search of his family roots, and never left. An established antiques dealer, he continued to ply his trade on the island, reflecting its maritime heritage. Three times a year, a container arrives full of treasures collected on trips back to England—local antiques are scarce, although the island's tradition of beachcombing and recycling continues to flourish, harvesting fragments of old wrecks, sometimes even the cargoes of doomed container ships. Huddled together in hamlets along the island's few roads, Ouessant's picturesque cottages were traditionally constructed from wood collected on the storm-washed foreshore. The resulting partition screens and carved furniture were painted to mask the mismatched timber. Paul has left his island home untouched, as a natural setting for his collection of seafaring objects—some still sourced from locals and mariners, each piece telling the story of a simple life lived at the edge of the world.

Simple objects evoking the lives and
memories of seafaring folk

In a neighboring house, converted to a tearoom, Paul displays a life-size half-hull from the harbor
in Lampaul, Ouessant's main town. Model boats, ship's lanterns, deck fittings, lifebelts, and portholes—
Paul's carefully sourced collection of maritime objects is a testimony to the lives of seafaring folk.
Other pieces speak of those left waiting ashore: minutely detailed dioramas, witches' balls in metallized
glass, touching ex-votos, and protective statues of the Virgin Mary (the sailors' *bonne mère*),
like those seen dotting the island's winding roads.

Down on the beach

LE CHÂTEAU DE SABLE
Guesthouse

France Ladouceur freely admits that life in Cavalaire-sur-Mer is an endless vacation. Her beachfront house is the last word in stylish living-on-sea. Anchored at the far end of Cavalaire beach, Le Château de Sable—transformed from the solid foundations of a 1960s villa—is one sandcastle that's here to stay. In a fairytale setting, it is a child's dream house for carefree vacations. With the help of her two daughters, France has created a timeless, effortlessly elegant setting, a bastion of serene calm. Bedrooms gaze out to sea from private balconies, and the hotel's drawing room extends into the garden, with huge tables and solid wooden benches lounging quietly beneath the umbrella pines. A path of stepping stones dots the grass, leading to a small gate that opens directly onto the beach, its carpet of white sand an open invitation to your morning dip. Or candlelit dinners of fine Provençal cuisine, served overlooking the sea in summer.

Canoe paddles, a model boat, a fisherman's stool, a panama hat, and a straw boater, reminding us that the sea is just around the corner. The stylish interior is a mix of flea-market finds and new pieces crafted from recycled materials, like the large dining-room table, made from broad wooden planks placed on trestles.

The decor is a haven of rustic charm, with essential modern comforts. The finest natural,
local materials blend with the gentle color scheme: a subtle harmony of vintage linen,
cotton or blended textiles, distressed wood, whitewash, rich polished leather,
and ethereal ironwork. For rainy days (they are few) a padded club armchair
or a *méridienne* covered in chocolate-colored linen stand waiting indoors.

By the light of the sea

Le Perche
A butterfly on the shoulder

VILLAGE DU VAL D'HUISINE
Antiques and collectibles

As one might expect, France's major roads are peppered with countless *brocantes* and *dépots-vente*, or consignment shops. Loudly proclaimed by signs and piles of hoardings, they form a disorderly queue along many routes popular among *brocante* dilettantes on their travels.

The national highway just outside Nogent-le-Rotrou is no exception to the rule. Taking over the site of a former service station, four *brocanteurs* have joined forces in a village in the Valley of the Huisne. Having cut their teeth in the Parisian markets of Vanves and Saint-Ouen, these four battle-worn musketeers now ply their trade in this pleasant bit of country in the Perche. All four have created their own little worlds in their shops in the "village": there's Marie, who goes in for curios, sophisticated vintage, and scullery and pantry furniture; and Philou, who has a remarkable nose for religious trinkets—from large-scale depictions of the Stations of the Cross down to humble crucifixes—though there are pagan gewgaws too, including a mighty collection of 1970s plastic costume jewelry.

72

Rather than merchants
in the temple, then, this
happy lot of eclectic
dealers together offer
bargain-hunters scouring
the national highways
a chance to make some
unexpected discoveries—
and indulge in a spot
of time travel.

If you're lucky, you might stumble across a wooden propeller from
who-knows-what lunatic UFO, a set of Napoleon III globes, or
an unbreakable wooden "Dejou" toy truck, which long ago you may
have wheeled around the living room yourself—you never know.
After all, the most rewarding journey any vintage-lover can make
is the one that goes back in time, to childhood.

Deepest Provence

LE MAS DOU PASTRE
Boutique hotel, gypsy caravans

It was twenty years ago at least—Albine and Maurice Roumanville remember it well. They have worked as antiques dealers, and tried their hands at other things, too. In the early 1990s, their parents left the family *mas*, its oldest stones dating back to the eighteenth century, at the foot of the Alpilles hills. To keep the house in the family, they decided to create a hotel, starting with just three rooms. Then six. Then their first gypsy caravan. In just five years, the hotel became a reference for the best in Provençal living. Truly a *hôtel de charme*, created by Albine and Maurice with a genuine sense of hospitality. "We did whatever felt right," says Albine. Bric-a-brac, vintage objects, and antiques are everywhere, of course. Furniture picked up in Provençal markets, collections of items found here and there: glass cloches and jars, zinc watering cans and jugs, and small flower paintings.

A collection of multicolored wine demijohns
from the 1950s adorns the sitting room.
Each bedroom has its own personality, underscored
with a particular color, a chestnut-wood
garden chair, a woven basket.

The garden is now home to three traditional
gypsy caravans: La Gitane, La Manouche, and
La Voyageuse, bought from traveling families,
and the director of a circus. The last word
in bohemian style.

An urge to chat

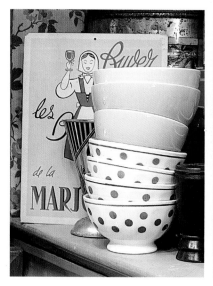

L'OBJET QUI PARLE...
Collectibles

I can safely say that my desire to write this book was kindled in the company of the friendly pair of eccentrics who run this place. L'Objet qui parle... sits between Pigalle and Abbesses, in the Paris of Amélie Poulain fame. A name, a shopfront, three walls, and that's it. Little more than a handkerchief—130 square feet perhaps—that Dominique and Guillaume reinvent every Monday when they return from their bargain hunting. Originally from Alsace, a region they often still scour, they always return with booty worthy of Ali Baba.

On a shelf cobbled together from wooden cotton reels—a neat bit of recuperation that was common enough in the textile-producing cities of northern and eastern France—is a motley stack of bowls, Viandox cups, old "Kub" stock-cube boxes, a wicker basket filled with etched glass test tubes.

All humor and tenderness, our two dealers compose these odds and ends into still lifes, making do with the blank stare of a puppet clown, a cuddly toy puppy, or one (of three) sardonic little piggies. As you excavate, your eye is drawn by kitsch ecclesiastical articles and other churchy knickknacks. Candlesticks, wedding bells, processional banners, nativity figures, and statues of angels rub shoulders with souvenirs from Lourdes and other holy curios—like the tiny brass hearts from the 1938 Marian Congress at Boulogne-sur-Mer, in which the pious would secrete their private hopes and prayers. Just one of the lovely stories that L'Objet qui parle... is willing to share with us.

Beachcombing bric-a-brac

LA LANGOUSTE BLEUE
Collectibles

Dominique and Jean-Pierre's delicious, beachfront bric-a-brac business is a cheery assortment of treasures, packed with vintage textiles and nightshirts, ornaments, children's toys, and folk art. Their home is as picturesque as the shop, and Dominique presides here with characteristic delight. The small Breton stone house has been transformed into an exquisite seaside cottage, surrounded by a rambling, luxuriant garden to share with family and friends—a place for sunbathing, dining by candlelight, chatting quietly with friends, enjoying an afternoon nap. Children dart here and there, shouting, laughing, playing. Further away, in a quiet corner, Jean-Pierre's office and private retreat is installed in a beach-style chalet. Everyone has their favorite spot, in the house and garden alike. But everyone gathers at the appointed time, to savor lunch served by Dominique, picnic style or seated around the huge dining table, for the assembled crew.

The kitchen is decorated in a bright
combination of yellows and greens,
inspired by points south (Provence, Morocco)
and the iconic colors of Dominique's
collection of Quimper earthenware—one
of her many passions.

Ships in bottles, boxes covered in shells,
terra-cotta figurines from L'Isle-Adam
or Villenauxe-la-Grande, works of folk art—
Dominique adores picturesque objects
and naïf art inspired by the seafaring life.

traditional

Of love and elbow grease

LES SARDINES AUX YEUX BLEUS
Guesthouse

Charlie Chaplin singing in *Limelight* couldn't have wished for a better place to stay when he hoped to be reincarnated as a sardine: "Oh for the life of a sardine,/ That is the life for me." Anna used to be a model, Olivier a photographer. They met on a shoot, the years passed, and one day they decided to turn a page and start a family. In the sweet-smelling scrubland of southern France, the young couple came across an isolated village with a crumbling seventeenth-century house that needed restoration from top to bottom. Using a good dose of elbow grease, augmented by knowledge gleaned from the entire collection of *Do-It-Yourself for Dummies*, Anna and Olivier set to work.

After four years, the house sparkled, and they were ready to welcome guests. A majestic staircase leads to a charming terrace, which in turn leads to three cool and colorful bedrooms. Outside, there is a lovely arbor, a pool, and an additional discrete duplex. Inside, colors are warm, objects trawled from secondhand shops in the countryside add a bohemian note, and lovely old household linens are a final touch of luxury. Oh yes, we did find out where the "sardines" in the guesthouse's name come from: a locksmith left a stamp in the shape of a sardine on the door fittings of the house. What we don't know is why their eyes are blue.

The language of flowers

LES ROSÉES
Guesthouse

On the Riviera, everyone understands the language of luxury hotels, yachts, and private beaches. The language of flowers is less widely known. If you want to learn it, head in the direction of Mougins, above Cannes. At nine in the morning, the sun already floods the garden where the dew has barely dried. There is no mystery about the source of inspiration for the name Kilpérick Lobet has chosen for this guesthouse. Les Rosées (morning dewdrops) abound here. The house is a four-century-old Provençal building. There are a few suites for guests: Isadora, Saint Marguerite, Serguey, and Saint Honorat each have a salon or boudoir.

As much attention is paid to your comfort as you would expect of a luxury boutique hotel, with bathrobes and fine bath accessories provided. But the spirit of the guesthouse remains artisanal, in the finest sense of the word, just like the work the owners put into decorating it. The muted, almost monastery-like atmosphere of certain rooms, with their rough walls, contrasts strikingly with the fine upholstery of the bed linens and drapes, all hand sewn in the family-run upholstery and interior-design studio next door, Les Ateliers de Mougins. One could live here as if one were on a Mediterranean island, far from the frivolities of the Riviera coast, appreciating the privacy the house affords. It's no surprise then that many of the guests are couples getting away from it all, celebrating a wedding anniversary or on honeymoon.

And the souvenirs taken away sometimes last forever—a young English couple who came to enjoy their last few days of freedom before the birth of their baby actually left with a little girl. Naturally enough, they named her Eva ... Rose!

An inviting home

LA MAISON DES LAMOUR
Bed-and-breakfast,
vacation cottages

Céline grew up here, in the Côtes d'Armor, where her parents Jeanne and Jean-Paul created a cheerful, bucolic retreat: the Char à Banc. An old mill, nestling at the bottom of a valley, renovated and restored over the years, a haven for families from far and wide. A place for lunch—a savory *potée* stew, or Breton pancakes; a place for pedal boats and pony rides. A place to stay and sleep, too, in the farmhouse next door, where Céline and Marc have labored to create a home-from-home for guests, friends, and their children. Around the square courtyard, each of the farm outbuildings has become a "guest house" open to the woods and fields. The main house reflects the couple's boundless talent and creativity, their flair for breathing new life into old objects, their insatiable passion for bric-a-brac and antique-hunting. From the entrance hall—dotted with sepia portraits—an ancient, patinated staircase leads to the former granary.

A streetlamp—salvaged from a street in Paris—hangs in the hallway
of the main house. Sliding metal panels open onto the dining room
and living room. Picture windows installed in the farm's rear walls look
onto the kitchen garden which provides fresh vegetables for residents
and diners at the Char à Banc!

Gray, beige, white, and natural light. The walls of the smaller, cramped rooms have been knocked through. Wells of light pierce the wooden floor of the granary, illuminating the space. Slatted wooden side panels from an old cart form a balustrade. Every space bursts with Céline and Marc's unusual, offbeat ideas, inspired by their instinct to reuse and reycle, and their many finds at country bric-a-brac sales.

The bedrooms are no exception—here, even stacks of old books and papers find new uses.
Faded paperbacks form a bedside table. Old novels, faded and foxed, become charming small pictures
while they wait for a new reader. Pages from a battered old school book are separated and hung
one by one to form a long, decorative frieze—a new chapter in the lively history of the Maison Lamour!

Le Perche
A rural retreat

LES PETITES FARIES
Vacation cottage, decoration

His Volvo is a familiar sight on the deep-set country roads of the Perche, southwest of Chartres. Behind the wheel is antiques dealer Arnaud de Saint-Martin, inveterate hunter of staircases, doors, and fireplaces. He adores the eighteenth century and fine natural materials. A chance real-estate advertisement brought him to a ruined *longère* in his native region: a dreamed-of idyll, a family home, a launchpad for new projects. The sale was speedily concluded, and the little farm began its metamorphosis. Flint walls were laid bare, some were knocked down. The surfaces were treated with limewash in the region's traditional yellow. New additions paid court to the existing, ancient house. The garden, enclosed by a hedge of pleached beech, was graced by a hideout for the children. Reawakened and restored, the house is now a gite, available to rent for country weekends.

In the living room, traditional board games stand ready for a rainy Sunday afternoon. Above a roaring fire, candles light up the elegant frame of a nineteenth-century overmantel. Arnaud, a dedicated *brocanteur*, ensures nothing goes to waste: the kitchen units were cut down from old doors and handles are fashioned from old cutlery. Upstairs, the old saloon-style doors from a defunct cinema, La Dernière Séance, find new life. A child's paradise!

Board games for a rainy day

In the master bedroom, a Napoleon III armchair has
been reupholstered in purple fabric. A shoemaker's
last has been transformed into a lamp base. Arnaud
is full of ideas for bringing old objects back to life.

A traditional family hotel

L'HÔTEL DES DEUX MERS
Hotel

Belle-Île floats on the horizon, and the Quiberon peninsula stretches out from the mainland to the very last landing stage, like an invitation to set sail, a foretaste of the bracing ocean air. Bordering the Côte Sauvage— the peninsula's celebrated, wild Atlantic coastline of spectacular cliffs and expansive beaches—the Hôtel des Deux Mers is a fine old hotel, built in the 1930s, in the heyday of the family seaside vacation. High ceilings, polished hardwood floors, a huge verandah, and a garden that reaches down to the beach—the Deux Mers has it all. Delphine and Mathieu Dubos fell in love with the building—and its setting—at first sight, bought it with little thought for the gargantuan task ahead, and dedicated themselves to bringing the place up to date. Bedrooms were extended to become family suites, floors were covered with sisal matting, dark wooden paneling was repainted in soft gray. The hotel's services were given a makeover, too, with a host of ideas for families from their very first season: picnic baskets on request, bicycles available to all guests, even a flotilla of sand yachts—the perfect way to enjoy the windswept beach nearby.

The huge communal dining room—the setting
for breakfast and afternoon tea—opens onto
the verandah at the rear of the hotel. Adirondack
chairs and benches piled with thick cushions
are the perfect setting for vacation reading
or a game of chess.

Simple furniture and antique-shop finds recreate the atmosphere of
a much-loved family vacation home. The guest rooms are furnished with
wicker armchairs, *bonnetières,* and cupboards patinated by a friend and
bric-a-brac dealer from La Trinité-sur-Mer. Rooms and communal spaces are
decorated in a palette of soft grays with subtle touches of color.

Walking in the dunes, feeling the wind in your hair, breathing the salty
sea air, flying a kite. After a trip to the beach, each hotel room
is a welcoming cocoon, a place to read or sit on the balcony,
watching the sun dip below the ocean horizon.

The ocean and the shore

L'ESPRIT DU CAP
Antiques, decoration

Now we've reached the ocean and the Bassin d'Arcachon hat nestles between the dunes of Pilat and Cap-Ferret and where Stéphane Bugot has established, right at the end of the spit, his most recent pied-à-terre. A descendant from a line of three generations of antique dealers, Bugot spent time at the Louvre (where the antique stores are) and then opened his first boutique at Saint-Cloud on the outskirts of Paris, before escaping into a career in luxury goods. His notion of luxury has changed now, too: the sea, a good book, a good sweater, and a good armchair. Hence *L'Esprit du Cap*, where even the sign comes as a surprise: ANTIQUITÉS – SPORTSWEAR.

There are sweaters obviously, but the label reads "handknit" and they are accompanied by a splendid panorama of coastal vintage wares. Paneled in faded blue painted pine, the "Spirit of the Cape" satisfies every desire for the ocean—whether you're an old sea dog or a landlubber. From yacht furniture to long-haul trunks, from solid captain's chairs to lanterns and other maritime necessities, in burnished copper and dark wood, naturally; there's a folding screen, a 1900s cane deckchair, a wardrobe in pitch pine, a bamboo console table for the stay-at-homes, and, on the walls—a further invitation to distant climes—a collection of pictures and seascapes, of which at least one will feature an ancient transatlantic steamship.

And, as a fitting end, there's the inevitable inkstand made of painted shells, mussels, scallops, and mother-of-pearl that betrays the nostalgic heart of the place.

Pure countryside

LA FERME DE MARIE-EUGÉNIE
Guesthouse

At the eastern reaches of Burgundy lies the Bresse area. Somewhere between the towns of Chalon-sur-Saône and Lons-le-Saunier, the road disappears into the mist covering the apparently deserted countryside, so famous for the gastronomical-quality chickens raised there. At the end of an unpaved road lies La Ferme de Marie-Eugénie. For a long time, this family farm was occupied only on weekends and during vacations. Then Dominique and Marie-Eugénie gave up their jobs in advertising in Paris to start anew in this remote country area. Dominique set to work, undertaking major remodeling of the outbuildings to transform them into guestrooms.

Marie-Eugénie got going on the decoration, hunting down objects and furnishings, avidly reading magazines, and scouring professional fairs. Summer arrived, and the farm was ready to open its doors to visitors. The way to get there was properly signposted, and the first guests appeared—from Belgium, Switzerland, and all over France. The couple was somewhat surprised to discover that their remote spot had suddenly become a center of attraction—thanks to the Internet, of course. But upon arrival, it's easy to see that there is nothing virtual about the charm of the place. What could be more real than the warm welcome that awaits you? The owners know the essentials of the good life. For starters, the cuisine is always generous: it includes, naturally, local chicken dishes, *jambon persillé* (the regional specialty of parsley-studded pressed ham), and a wonderful terrine that Marie-Eugénie always has in stock for unexpected guests.

A gastronomic ecolodge

GRAINE ET FICELLE
Bed-and-breakfast (and more)

The donkeys are named Estaban, Chiquito, Poncho, and Lila. The cow goes by the name of Roquette. Isabella is Italian—from Rome—a young, energetic former stylist who has retreated to Saint-Jeannet from life in the big city. Back to nature—the simple life, in the herb-scented backcountry of the Côte d'Azur. On the site of an ancient, stone shepherd's hut, Isabella has created a house open to the region's dazzling light, and an organic farm. A madcap scheme that is gradually taking root: a kitchen garden, free-range animals, a new life. Guided farm visits for children and school groups, a guesthouse, cooking classes, wine tastings. A hectic schedule! And a host of projects and plans in the offing. Isabella's kitchen has been featured on TV— her past is catching up with her!

In the mountains north of Nice, Isabella's home boasts stunning views of the distant Mediterranean.
The kitchen—the heart of the farm—was the first space to be completed. Since then the operation has grown,
little by little: a natural swimming pool, a greenhouse, a jam-making workshop. Peppers, zucchini, and green beans
are favorite ingredients for Isabella's exceptional vegetable preserves, in huge demand from Nice's top chefs—who
have become clients and friends, sharing their expertise through cooking classes offered at the farm.

Fine cuisine, to the letter

Isabella's first visitors came to sample her organic farmhouse cooking, learn a new recipe, the tricks of the trade. The lunches got longer—now guests come to spend a day in the country, a night or two in one of the guest rooms, or the ecolodges: comfortable tented pavilions installed nearby (meals are taken at the farm). There are even plans for a new ecohouse on the site.

Île de Ré
Ephemeral wisdom

LA TREILLE MARINE
Collectibles

On this island devoted to all things decorative, antique hunting has become a way of life and each village on Île de Ré has plenty to choose from. There's the Bigorneau Langoureux at La Flotte, Campani at Saint-Martin, Galerie Kahn, Côté Jardin, Boutique, and 20—where one can grab a drink as well—at Ars. Off the beaten path, however, one comes across La Treille Marine. Danielle pays no heed to the weather or time of the day, and throws back her shutters whenever she fancies. So, La Treille has no opening hours as such, and you just have to be lucky to enter this bohemian (not to say eccentric) little world. A born storyteller, our brocanteuse creates touching scenarios in which every element is selected and positioned with immense care.

Everything has a role:
for Easter weekend,
for instance, Danielle
arranges a meeting
between a scuffed Christ,
a chocolate rabbit, and
a bird and some eggs
fallen from a nest. When
the moment comes to
open up shop, however,
the storybook is closed
again, because Danielle
reuses each figure in
another decoration,
so that its tale vanishes
without trace.

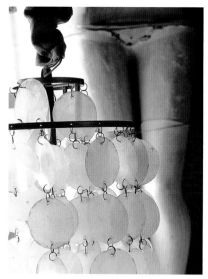  

The only evidence left of the "bride's story" she concocted out of a disembodied pair
of wooden legs and a bit of taffeta, adorned with some rice grains and a few pearly pendants,
is a fleeting memory recorded in a misty photograph. One can imagine a whole life unfolding
in a composition made up of a photograph of a communicant, some medallions, a rosary,
a music score, and a crucifix, all pinned to a partition constructed of scraped-down floorboards.
After briefly communing with nature in her secret garden—an authentic Île de Ré plot filled, as
one might expect, with evocative set pieces—Danielle sets out once again into the countryside
to track down materials for a new page in her very personal Book of Hours.

In the shade of the pine trees

LA MAISON DU BASSIN
Hotel, restaurant

Fifteen years ago, Nicole and William Joinau took a gamble that paid off—realizing their wild dream of converting an old hotel, on a whim and a prayer. The building proved a sound starting point: completed in 1899, it has been adopted by successive generations of vacationers on the Cap Ferret peninsula. When the Joinaus took over, they dedicated themselves to creating a stylish travelers' retreat, a veritable home-from-home. Soon, the blue-painted wooden verandah was entwined with wisteria. The interior, refurbished and decorated with flea-market finds and thoughtful extra touches over the years, is suffused with the timeless style of a much-loved family seaside retreat. The guest rooms, terrace, bistro, and bar offer a delightfully intimate, friendly atmosphere, and the hotel is a favorite venue for friends playing *pétanque* or for couples—from Paris to New York—holding romantic wedding ceremonies. The ultimate seal of approval.

Echoing the beach huts and chalets of Cap Ferret, wood is an essential feature
at the Maison du Bassin—untreated, varnished, painted, tinted, or lime washed,
it characterizes every corner of this atmospheric building. An old-fashioned
calendar hangs in the entrance hall. Vintage tennis rackets in faded cotton covers
and wooden frames stand as if waiting for a game.

From the wooden doors to the seascapes hanging on the walls, much of the furniture
and decor comes from L'Esprit du Cap, an antiques and bric-a-brac emporium run
by the Joinaus' neighbor and friend—a treasured source of new objects, from
a collection of nautical pennants to a painting of a storm at sea. Each of the hotel's
eleven rooms is unique and individually decorated, to the delight of its regular guests.

A flair for the *mise en scène*

JUSTIN DE PROVENCE
Guesthouse

Eugénie and Victor, Thérésia and Marius, Augusta and Léon, Augustine and Achille, Marie-Jeanne and… Justin. No, this is not a list of the latest first names for babies in France. These typically Provençal names, each pair of which is given to one of the bedrooms in this guesthouse, are all of members of Isabelle's family. Justin was her grandfather, and he bought this stone shepherd's shelter in 1927. But he would barely recognize it now, for Isabelle and Philippe, her husband, have imprinted their joyfulness and sunny natures—in short, all the characteristics of Provence—on the house. Justin de Provence, which lies languidly on the plain between the city of Orange with its famed Roman ruins and the steep lacy mountains known as Les Dentelles de Montmirail, embodies their love of interior decoration.

Multicolored, patterned cement tiling and whitewashed walls are set off by an amazing collection of objects sourced at various antique and junk stores. Curios fill the house and spill over into the garden. There's an old bicycle with a basket and a wooden handle, a pile of old-fashioned enameled advertising signs, and more. The owners' generosity also overflows when it comes to well-being. In addition to the outdoor pool, much appreciated in this hot dry climate, the couple have just built one indoors. Created with an art-deco ambience, the new pool abuts a relaxation room, for unwinding in peace. It's an ideal place to lie with your loved one and dream about how to bring a taste of this lifestyle back home with you. Le Parfait Amour (Perfect Love) is the name of the bistro Philippe runs aside the guesthouse and opening onto its gardens, a scene worthy of one of the many Marcel Pagnol books and, later, films—such as *Jean de Florette* and *Manon des Sources*—set in the area.

In a field of flowers

PETITES MAISONS DANS LA PRAIRIE
Bed-and-breakfast, vacation cottages

It's a family affair: we've met Céline and Marc, owners of that essential country retreat, the Char à Banc. Now meet Corentin and Liz, at Plélo, a blissful hamlet nestling between the Atlantic and the lush Brittany countryside. With a nod to childhood memories, the couple have named their gîtes the "little houses on the prairie": seven cozy holiday cottages surrounded by a farm, fields of cows, meadows of tall grass dotted with cosmos flowers. Choose from Rose, Florence, Marie, Louise, Joséphine, Anne, and Jeanne—each stone cottage is named for a grandmother, a great aunt, or a dear neighbor. And each of the seven "queens of hearts" has actually lived in one of these traditional Breton longhouses. Corentin's mother Jeanne was even born here. When Irish-born Liz arrived from Cork to perfect her French, she stole his heart away.

Seven little houses, full of delights

Corentin and Liz began by renovating one of the cottages as their home. Corentin took charge of the farm and its animals, and little by little each cottage was restored. The walls are insulated with natural limewash and hemp from the fields; farm objects have been recycled, pieces of furniture picked up here and there. Liz brings her personal charm and creativity to the decor. Painted wooden floors, checkered tiles, doors pierced with a scattering of cut-out hearts, garlands of lights, and always a bouquet of fresh wildflowers. An irresistible call to pack your bags and take to the fields.

An organic oasis

LES ORANGERIES
Hotel, restaurant

Angers, Poitiers, Limoges. Towns that too many travelers know only as signposts off France's southbound routes, choked with summer vacationers heading for the Mediterranean. But some will turn off here, where the road falls into step with the valley of the river Vienne, and head for the village of Lussac-les-Châteaux, the birthplace of Madame de Montespan. An oasis. A mirage, perhaps? No, ideed: the village is home to France's first officially recognized ecohotel, a gem discovered by pioneering guests back in the late 1990s, when Olivia and Jean-Philippe launched a charming hotel in a seventeenth-century house belonging to the family, dedicated to sustainable development and a certain art of fine living. Jean-Philippe has fond memories of family vacations here as a child. Now an architect, he took charge of renovating and refurbishing the hotel, taking account of the necessary rules and regulations (of course), but also his personal skills and beliefs. Materials were sourced locally, often recycled, the walls were insulated with hemp, and the interior surfaces were coated with limewash colored using natural pigments. Each new extension or enhancement follows the same philosophy—the guiding principle of daily life in this special place, too.

The decor is Olivia's domain. The hotel's lively chatelaine is a fervent devotee of sustainable tourism and development: vintage furniture and objects are hunted down and restored, fabrics and drapes feature warm, vivid colors. Motifs give a discreet nod to the orange trees that fill the hotel's landscaped gardens.

Olivia's commitment to sustainable tourism is shared by the entire hotel team, including the young chef, whose superb dishes use seasonal local produce—mainly organic—from nearby kitchen gardens.

Elementary objects

MAMIE GÂTEAUX
Collectibles, tea room

It's back to the pioneer days of the department store.
We're on rue du Cherche-Midi, a stone's throw from the
famous Bon Marché emporium. Madame holds sway
in the tearoom (hence, *Mamie-Gâteaux*) where light
lunches pull in the crowds, while Monsieur orchestrates the
adjacent *brocante* "corner shop" that refreshes its display
each season. If the school term is under way, then rows of
wooden or metal teachers' tables and pupils' desks spring
up everywhere, as if this were a school museum.

Plumier

le rossignol   chante

le rossignol   chante

le rossignol   chante

le rossignol   chante

le printemps est un des qu

le printemps   est

le printemps   est

le printemps est une

With a pencil case complete with inkstand, an exercise book inscribed with a hundred lines, a well-traveled geography textbook, a checkered apron or a graying smock, one is whisked back to the (good old) days of Mr. Chips. Luckily, the pigeonholes in a hardware storage cabinet are filled with plenty of fun things for recess: a jump rope or a bag of marbles filled with "shooters," "taws," "agates," and "steelies." Teatime beckons, so at the rear of the store Hervé Duplessis has rebuilt a postwar kitchen. From the venerable enameled iron stove to the nest of spice boxes, from the genteel chromolithograph to the dollhouse kitchen, everything here is carefully calculated to take one back to happier, simpler days.

School posters

Issued on a huge scale in the postwar period by the French teachers' confederation—the Maison des Instituteurs—and by publishers such as Rossignol and Bourrelier, schoolroom posters sometimes make a welcome appearance at garage sales in the country. At *Mamie-Gâteaux* they inevitably form part of the decor, with some rarer specimens such as botanical plates from the era of Napoleon III as well as science, history, and language posters, or others showing scenes from everyday life. Illustrated with talent and individuality, by for instance, René Bresson and Hélène Poirié, they often cast a candid light on the history of an age that many remember with nostalgia. There are the gardens (Luxembourg or the Tuileries?) with their endless daily parades, or else the madcap adventures of Aline and Rémi on the colored posters used for pronunciation training, where it's all "*ba be bi bo bu.*"

In search of lost time

AU TEMPS RETROUVÉ
Guesthouse

Tea with apple crêpes, and rich cakes of chestnut, raspberry, and agar. All year round, Florence serves delicious brunches and afternoon teas in her elegant house at the tip of the Île de Ré—a soothing haven of hospitality, dedicated to recapturing the slower pace of a bygone age. A place of Proustian atmosphere and attention to detail, both carefully choreographed and delightfully spontaneous. A former dancer and a seasoned traveler from India to Morocco, Florence has dropped anchor in the island village of Ars-en-Ré, renovating her home using simple, natural materials: recycled pine floorboards line the walls, insulated with lime wash and hemp, while the floors are covered with traditional cement tiles by Agnès Emery. Furniture and everyday objects are picked up at bric-a-brac and antiques markets, for fun, old-fashioned comfort, and that indefinable feel-good factor.

Tanned leather, hemp, linen, and fine embroidery

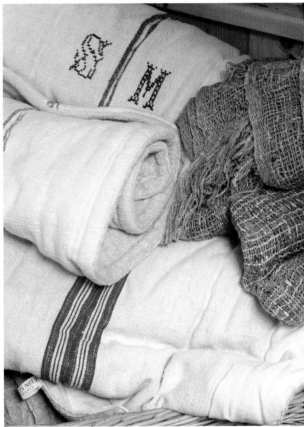

Canvas, woven hemp bags, and plump, finely embroidered cushions are piled
on beds and sofas. Found objects—from a collection of dried starfish to a slip-cast tea service,
glass cloches, a tinkling chandelier, and a simple pair of vintage slippers—are dotted
from room to room, creating a delightful, harmonious atmosphere, lulled by a soundtrack
of retro jazz courtesy of Chet Baker.

A diaphanous veil floats on the frame of
a four-poster bed, against a backdrop
of natural, chalk-textured colors. In the
neighboring bedroom, the bathroom is open to
the wider space, offset by a dark, muted purple.

Romantic

In good company

LA SEIGNEURIE
Bed-and-breakfast

Just getting here is a joy in itself. As the last stop on the traditional pilgrimage to the bay of Mont Saint-Michel, La Seigneurie stands serenely behind high granite walls. Built in the twelfth century, the original house has been extended, transformed, demolished, and reconstructed over the centuries. The setting is a haven of charm, and its history is fascinating, too—Françoise and Michel have breathed new life into the house, inherited from a long line of corsairs and shipbuilders from nearby Saint-Malo. Far from submitting meekly to the immutable heritage of its massive stone walls, Françoise—a former antiques dealer— has tackled it head-on, with taste and flair, due respect, and an extra dose of tough love. A passionate collector of eighteenth-century decorative arts, she has thrown herself into the task of creating a comfortable, contemporary, ephemeral interior. The woodwork and walls (inside and out) are often repainted with fresh colors; and a new bedroom is opening soon, in the gardener's annex.

Scallop shells, the traditional gift of thanks left
by pilgrims on the route to Santiago de
Compostela, are pressed into the walls or displayed,
here, on a delicate wire support. Françoise and
Michel take a playful approach to decoration,
finding new uses for old objects, like the kitchen
table, mounted on the base of an old church pulpit.

Saffron yellow, terra-cotta red, faded blue: Françoise experiments with her Farrow
and Ball paints, mixing new shades of her own for the Seigneurie's woodwork,
inside and out. In the bedrooms, an old panettone box, compressed cardboard
suitcases, lengths of vintage linen hung like bridal veils, and embroidered,
monogrammed sheets add to the hotel's gentle charm.

In the Grande Cour suite, the alcove bed nestles beneath a mezzanine lined
with recycled wood paneling from a local church. Françoise accommodates
solid pieces of nineteenth- and twentieth-century furniture, placing an Imperial
bench alongside a pair of elegant, upright metal chairs brought back from
the States—like timeless treasures displayed on a traveler's return
from an around-the-world voyage.

Strains of Erik Satie

LE CLOS BOURDET
Guesthouse

Fan and Jean-Claude Osmont were already well-known in Honfleur. Anyone who went on an outing along the Grâce Coast, for a walk around the docks, or a stroll in the twisting streets of the small town invariably finished with a stop for tea and cakes at their teashop, La Petite Chine. After twenty-five years of running it, they decided to make a change, settling in to another cozy place, Le Clos Bourdet. The building, an eighteenth-century manor house, has lofty views over the town of Honfleur but retains the warm friendliness that prevailed in their teashop, topped with a good dose of imagination.

The notes of Éric Satie's melodies seem to float up from the piano in the living room. (Satie was born in Honfleur). The atmosphere is gentle, but the tone is quirky. Walls and wood are painted in whimsical pastels—"seaside" blue, chocolate mauve, or soft yellow, depending on how the changing Normandy skies illuminate them.

What is constant throughout the house is a marked taste for mixing and matching aesthetics and eccentricity: shiny chandeliers, leopard-print fabrics, collections of unique objects hunted down in bric-a-brac stores, and, everywhere, Jean-Claude's large-format black-and-white photos. Even though they acknowledge that they owe something to places they've seen on their many voyages away from their home grounds—like the Villa Saint-Louis in Lourmarin in the Lubéron and the Comptoir d'Aubrac in Saint-Chély d'Aubrac—Jean-Claude and Fan have made the Clos Bourdet a unique place. And sure to please anyone seeking to relish the idyllic scenes of Honfleur that Monet once put onto canvas.

A place for daydreaming

LA MAISON
Guesthouse

The south of France is thrilling: extravagant, exuberant, and eccentric all at once. But it also has a mysterious side, and this house, tucked away in one of those enchanting villages of the Gard in Provence, plays on this duality. The eighteenth-century building, located on the peaceful church square, only reveals its secrets to those who cross its threshold. Laid out at the foot of a hundred-year-old linden tree, its terrace garden overlooks the Uzège region. With its palm trees, red wrought-iron furniture, and pretty table of potted plants, it's a perfect place for daydreaming.

La Maison knows how to breathe deeply and entices its occupants to do so as well. Its owners, Pierre Berringer and Christian Vaurie, have traveled through Asia and the Americas, and have transmitted the spirit of their voyages with subtlety throughout their house. After having run a guesthouse farther north in Touraine for seventeen years, Pierre entrusted a local interior designer, Richard Goullet, with enlivening his new spot in the sunny south. Lacquer paint and whitewash, pale blue and warm gold, azure floor tiles and stained cement—an entire palette of techniques complement Goullet's artistry.

Adding his own creations to furniture discovered in antique shops and flea markets,
the decorator has turned the house into a gleaming canvas that makes the most of the light
and shadow of Provence. La Maison has been making its own little tour of the world in
the press of late and has become a meeting place for travelers from the four corners
of the earth. Its owners adore hosting all these people—though they still set aside
a few months in winter to travel themselves.

Sweet dreams

UN CŒUR TRÈS NATURE
Bed-and-breakfast

This former silkworm-breeding establishment, tucked away in Liouc, one of the oldest hamlets in the Gard department in southern France, has been transformed into a cocoon of tranquillity. Surrounded by natural scenery, this haven of peace is just a short drive away from major historical and cultural cities like Nîmes, Uzès, and Montpellier. With the help of her husband, Laetita has patiently restored the country house, transforming the rooms into treasure troves of carefully collected birdcages, charmingly timeworn pieces of furniture, decorated windowpanes, and as many hearts scattered around as your heart could desire, to remind you of the name of this guesthouse, which means "a very natural heart."

Laetitia has used the gentle warmth of wood and wicker to weave the right atmosphere for enjoying a complete break, away from it all. She does her utmost to make sure you can follow the instruction stenciled on one wall: *REVER*. Dream!

Bordeaux
From maxi to mini

LE PASSAGE SAINT-MICHEL
Antiques and collectibles

Bordeaux. The elegant capital of the southwest is experiencing a shake-up, with the quaysides undergoing a facelift, and whole districts being pedestrianized: it's now a place to saunter. Close to the Garonne river, the place Saint-Michel has lost nothing of its soul, though. Cosmopolitan and spawned from a tradition of craft and commerce, the market attracks the usual dose of antique hunters, strollers, and junk dealers. In front of the flea market, the Passage Saint-Michel offers a mixed bunch of stands over several stories.

Laurence's stand at the entrance—with tons of sculpture ranging from the monumental to the minuscule (like this battalion of Orientalist miniatures)—gives a taste of the time travel to come. Is it bric-a-brac, or a real antique? It's hard to tell as, eyes peeled, one crisscrosses this vintage "department store"—it now extends into a hangar once belonging to the Giffrer firm—that has been revamped by three retro addicts. Among the apparent pandemonium, the personality of each comes through: there's Ludovic, a former graphic designer, who presents a highly idiosyncratic cabinet of curiosities; Laurent, whose explosive decors can also be experienced at his gallery on the Île de Ré; and Jamel, who schleps his stock of industrial wares to the Quinconces fair, the huge biannual junket for *brocanteurs* from the southwest.

Tools and materials

Rarely escaping the wrath of demolition contractors, old building materials are becoming increasingly rare. For every ceramic basin or batch of cement tiles saved, how many cast-iron baths are shattered by a sledgehammer? How many iron railings and walls have been flattened by a bulldozer? It's a cruel, cruel world. And, for salvagers and secondhand dealers alike, building materials are as troublesome as they are hard to take down, transport, and revamp. So, turning regretfully away from a pair of oaken doors, a garden statue, or an entire stone mantelpiece, one settles for less weighty wonders, such as an ornamental pelmet (a single piece of which would be enough to decorate a wall in a reception room) or these masonry trowels still caked in dried plaster that might make an original corner shelf, or a set of resin pots that would impart a modestly elegant touch to any balcony.

Paris
The delicate scent of yesteryear

L'HEURE BLEUE
Antiques and collectibles

Ah! That magic moment. Martine and Vincent have a thing about dusk, the gloaming—the "blue twilight hour." So in their little shop, which recently closed its doors, time was precious, so much so that they had installed their own lunar calendar. Every month and a half (on the dot), the decor got a facelift. When springtime arrived, it morphed into a Paris garden hideaway. Outside were earthenware jars, pots, shovels, pitchers, gardening books, dried flowers, and growing racks, while behind the shutters an inviting landscape awoke beneath the starry glow of a vast teardrop chandelier.

This lasted until the next shake-up, which might see a romantic castle appear, or the cosy cocoon of one's home after a long time away, the heartwarming interior of a chalet in Alsace, or, in January—that traditional month for all things white—opulent heaps of bright linen and jute.

Naturally romantic

LA MAISON DU BAILLI
Private home

Bayeux is famous for its long tapestry celebrating the Norman conquest of England by the French duke Guillaume (William the Conqueror). In the sixteenth century, the local bailiff lived here, midway between the regional capital at Bessin, and the beaches of the Côte de Nacre (the "mother-of-pearl coast"). The house has a rich history. Geneviève and Francis visited and bought it in the space of just twenty-four hours. Moving to the country from the western Paris suburb of Rambouillet, they originally planned to settle in the Pays d'Auge. But they weren't looking for a thatched cottage or second home. Both fell in love with La Maison du Bailli—a typical, elegant Bessin mansion, with its carriage house, cider barn, and stables, renovated by a previous English owner. All that needed changing was the decor. To brighten the austere facade, Geneviève called in a young artist from the Beaux-Arts to create a series of trompe l'oeil yew trees on the walls of Creully stone—bringing the garden right up the house. And that's the key to this delightful home, whose serene gardens are discovered beyond its high entrance arch. A sense of tranquility that seduced Geneviève and Francis, happy to live here in all seasons.

The interior is filled with Geneviève's
bric-a-brac finds and restored pieces, from
Louis XIII to industrial chic, repainted and arranged
by the *maîtresse de maison*—something
she loves doing. Right now, she's considering
a more contemporary look.

Ce soir ou jamais, Petite chérie—each bedroom bears the name of a fragrance.
Geneviève leaves subtle clues, phrases dotted here and there, handwritten
on pebbles lying in trails, like breadcrumbs on a forest path.

A hidden gem

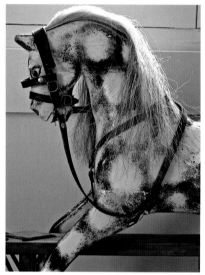

MA MAISON DE MER
Bed-and-breakfast

How many of us have dreamed of a life by the sea, sharing our time between the beach and the garden? Emma and Phillip Hutchison actually took the plunge. But for all that, they cannot be said to be on vacation all year round. They arrived from Yorkshire in 2004 to discover their house by the sea—which is what the name Ma Maison de Mer signifies—on what's known as the Coast of Beauty (la Côte de Beauté), near Royan. This house, which dates from the 1920s when sea resorts were at the height of fashion, is set amid pine trees just a few minutes away from the Conche des Platins. It had initially been a hotel—the very first hotel in Saint-Palais-sur-Mer—before it became a guesthouse, ably run by Emma and Phillip.

Even though they have finished remodeling, they have not stopped making improvements. With its white floorboards, sea-rush mats, fine net drapes, and lovely model boats hunted down in antique stores, this guesthouse is almost like being at sea, and just what one seeks for an ideal beach vacation.

The sea as a garden

UNE CHAMBRE D'HÔTES À DAHOUËT
Bed-and-breakfast

A private house, sheltered (say the locals) by the fabled microclimate of the Baie de Saint-Brieuc, on Brittany's north coast. A place for family vacations, where generations meet for the long summer break. Sailing school, rock-pooling for shellfish, catching lobsters in pots, tennis tournaments, a round of golf, hikes along the coastal path (the Sentier des Douaniers), high tides, and crumbling sandcastles. Marie-Claude and Alain have created the perfect family vacation house, and their own seaside home. With its clapboard façade and English-style bay and sash windows, wooden verandah, and balconies inspired by the architecture of the region's grand seaside villas, the building is flooded with natural light. The broad terrace, sheltered from the prevailing wind (and prying eyes), is a relaxing haven in all weathers. A place where guests are content to while away the hours, dreaming that maybe one day they could live nearby.

The huge bookcases were made to measure by
a joiner friend, for alcoves either side of
the fireplace (a flea-market find). A leather club
armchair and Lloyd Loom chairs offer their owner,
Alain, a well-deserved chance to relax—he built
the house himself, from scratch.

On a background of changing shades of gray, seashells and ceramics complement the many charming objects around the room–including an antique globe and oyster baskets gathered from bric-a-brac sales, which are as common to the region as fishing trips!

Shells, majolica, and *petit blanc* figurines

Stormy gray, wine-dark purple, pale blue-gray, or turquoise. As a counterpoint to the immaculate white finish of traditional *petit blanc* figurines from the Quimper earthenware factory, Marie-Claude Pelé gives free rein to her love of color, with an ebullient palette extending out into the garden. Planted with roses, agapanthus, palm trees, and seaside flora, the abundant flower beds encapsulate the house's serene sense of well-being, close to the living garden of the sea.

Picardy
A fresh start

LE 33 or LA MAISON DE GOUMY
Private home

Trente-trois. Thirty-three. At the risk of stating the obvious, "3" is a fetish figure at this guesthouse. So many owners of guesthouses have decided to leave their former lives to start over again. Naturally, Florence, owner of Le 33, has had three other lives. Her first belongs to the past: a career in Paris, small children, and a family house in L'Isle-Adam north of the French capital. Already a desire for country life was beginning to reveal itself. Near her home, Van Gogh's landscapes of Auvers-sur-Oise, the forests and valleys of the Vexin area, beloved to Monet, and the verdure of the Picardy area tipped the country-city scales and led her to her second life: running an old, country hotel that had cast its spell on her.

In (three) waves of a trowel and with a palette of tricks, it was transformed into a guesthouse—the guesthouse Florence had been dreaming of owning. Because she loved traveling; because, above all, she loved design, her own design. Inspired by a mélange of Gustavian style from Sweden, Flemish colors, and universal design pieces, plus her own insatiable desire to collect and display. As time-consuming as this is, she still finds time for a third life, one she leads under the blogger name of "Goumy." Thanks to Goumy, Florence can always be in two places at once, running the guesthouse while writing a chronicle of the everyday events of her life, and her decorating ideas and advice.

A whimsical fugue

LA PETITE FUGUE
Private home

This is a novel little tune that evokes the lapping of the Loire River. When they hit forty, Michel and Michelle decided to leave their careers in engineering and marketing on the banks of the Seine behind them to set up a home on the banks of the Loire. What they imagined would be just temporary—they called it La Parenthèse (The Parenthesis or Interlude)—left them anchored in the city of Blois. After a few arpeggios, they started Le Jardin Secret (The Secret Garden), an almost-private dining establishment for just fifteen people, with a hotel bedroom "just in case." The first few bars of their little fugue were already composed.

ALBUM-SOUVENIR

CHATEAUX
DE LA LOIRE

After visiting no fewer than one-hundred-and-fifty houses, they finally unearthed their rare gem, nestling on the banks of the Loire. It is a distinguished house, with high ceilings and original parquet flooring. The elegant decoration—cinnamon-colored linens and velvet throws—strikes just the right note. A short walk from the center of Blois, the house is not far from the famous châteaus of Azay-le-Rideau and Amboise, the wine route and cellars of the Loire region, and the intriguing Petrified Caves of Savonnières. Michel and Michelle will give you expert advice on where to go in this fascinating region. They also know when it's time to unwind around their dining table, tying their aprons back on and composing delightful menus, replete with special recipes and gourmet surprises.

Where time stands still

LE DONJON
Antiques and collectibles,
vacation cottage

In search of paradise, some might dream of a Moorish castle in Spain. Antiques dealer and gourmet Laure Chopy found her ideal *castillo* in the Normandy town of Trouville: a townhouse formerly owned by a gentleman by the fitting name of Paradis. Le Donjon was built in the late nineteenth century, at the heart of Trouville's winding streets and flowery seafront. The tall white building echoes the Moorish style popular at the time, decked with balconies and terraces gazing out to the misty ocean horizon. Divided into separate dwellings, the building today houses Laure's unconventional antiques emporium, a vacation apartment, and her private home, occupying the grand reception rooms of the original villa, on the upper floor. Subtle, Gustavian colors offset French furnishings from Louis XV to the Empire period, dotted with displays of Laure's myriad collections of objects. Like a collector's cabinet of curiosities, shellfish and sea fans are displayed in a *globe de mariée* (a glass cloche once used to display a bride's wedding bouquet) and a bouquet of dried hydrangea blooms decorates a Medici vase, suffused by the soft, bohemian light of the Normandy coast.

In the bedroom and living room, the owner's
collections are displayed on fine pieces of
eighteenth-century painted furniture bought
in Italy. A pair of period figurines stands
conspiratorially close, as if holding a private
conference. A single starfish, placed beneath
a delicate glass dome, completes the scene.

Timeless charm

LA MAISON DOUCE
Hotel, tea room

Time out. The news of the day can wait. Here, all that matters is an enchanting island home, a retreat from the world beyond. Catherine and Alain dropped everything to come and live here, acquiring the house ten years ago and changing very little since then—just enough to make the most of what was already there. Trips to the attic produced aged floorboards, an outsize wooden cupboard. The soul of the house laid bare. Visitors to the island village of Saint-Martin-de-Ré, midway along France's Atlantic seaboard, discover La Maison Douce with delight, in the maze of streets that make up its historic quarter. Dating from the eighteenth and nineteenth centuries, the building comprises a guesthouse and the owners' home, both opening onto a romantic garden—the setting for lazy afternoon teas in summer. Each guest room is a cocoon of soft colors, filmy fabrics, and heavy, luxurious linens. In the sitting room, Catherine and Alain have chosen rich colors for the walls (changing the scheme when the mood takes them), against which empty frames hang dreaming of unseen pictures, beyond.

In the beginning, Catherine and Alain created a guesthouse, with a handful
of simply furnished bedrooms painted in shades of camel, ash gray, violet,
chocolate, and white. The decor plays on juxtapositions of color and trompe
l'oeil, finished with a fine filet in a darker, contrasting shade. Other rooms were
renovated around the garden, and the house became a hotel, losing none
of its original, timeless charm.

LE PHARE DE RÉ

JOURNAL D'INTÉRÊT LOCAL, D'ANNONCES ET D'AVIS DIVERS

Cette semaine, notre
supplément

... sur les étals

Bathing beauties

LE CLOS JOSÉPHINE
Guesthouse

Vacations at Saint-Briac follow a timeless ritual. During the Belle Époque, travelers visiting the Côte d'Emeraude to bathe in the briny would gather on their first evening for dinner at the Auberge de la Croix Rouge. Now, the same building has been transformed by Françoise and her son Mathieu into a colorful, stylish guesthouse. After a full year of building work and refurbishment, the interior of this typical Breton inn has been completely remodeled and redecorated, bringing a touch of classic New England style to the north coast of Brittany. At the back of the house, in place of the old dining room, a huge verandah opens onto the garden and pool, gleaming with emerald light—a tempting alternative to the region's sweeping beaches. As a gentle reminder, each room is named after one of the ten within reach of this delightful seaside resort, including Grande and Petite Salinette, Le Bechet, La Garde, and Le Port Hue.

The walls are covered with whitewashed wainscoting dotted with vintage paintings
and family portraits, evoking the golden age of France's merchant navy,
and voyages to far-flung lands. Voyages that have inspired Françoise's distinctive
style, incorporating flea-market finds like ships' gangway doors, model boats,
or a small Louis Vuitton suitcase.

As a counterpoint to the level horizon traced by the paneling and bedheads,
the house's chairs and armchairs are covered with deckchair-striped fabrics
in colors redolent of the coastal landscapes of Brittany.

Vintage sheets, fine linen and embroidery,
translucent curtains, loose covers,
and cashmere throws: Le Clos Joséphine
is a haven of cocooning.

Paris

With a seasoned patina

VERT-DE-GRIS
Antiques

She may have chosen "Verdigris" as her byline, but Élisabeth Brac de la Perrière has more than one pigment on her palette. Superficially austere with a color scheme dominated by the muted tones of beige, green, brown, and, inevitably, gray, this refined setting merely adds luster to her displays. For ten years now, people have been picking up Gustavian-style furniture here on a regular basis. Subtle patinas, sanded or scrubbed wood, rusted handles and fittings all speak volumes for Élisabeth's undeniable talent; she is able to give zest to a chifforobe or a set of nineteenth-century chairs and dresser by adroitly adding that perfect and surprising accessory.

A natty footstool, some silver hotel tableware, a stack of medical textbooks from the 1800s, cast-iron plant pots, an architect's plan in faded ink, a basket filled with hooks and cream-colored shells, the bust—both grave and angelic—of a young Roman, a bizarre turquoise gable finial.

Élisabeth has a wonderful knack for that special finishing touch, for that affectionate detail, but also for concocting that alchemical moment when an old object meets its future purchaser. For, in the end, in life everything depends on meeting the right person.

Green horizons

LE RELAIS DE ROQUEFEREAU
Bed-and-breakfast,
vacation cottages

Nathalie has left town. Born into the fifth generation of a family of Parisian gallerists, she set out at the end of the 1990s to rediscover the landscapes of her childhood vacations. The Lot valley, Penne d'Agenais, a rich blend of nature and history. Here, she began a new life. In this rural setting, buying art isn't a high priority, so the gallerist turned antiques dealer. The green horizons of her daily drive became a part of life. And here, at the head of a small valley, she found this austere, majestic, beautiful building. The old medieval inn was solidly built, but the interior had suffered. After two years of work, Roquefereau was reborn. The new owner has opened gites and a bed-and-breakfast. Slate, linen, asphalt, pebbles—Nathalie has a feel for natural materials. Her home is clad in soft, subtle grays, enlivened here and there with touches of color—a painted canvas, an object— essential souvenirs of her former life, and her travels.

Roquefereau is serene and elegant, in its soft, pale palette of gray, taupe,
and charcoal, offset by white paint and limewash. A setting for a slower pace,
where small details are observed and appreciated: glass pendants, old jewelry,
small pictures that tell a story. Outside, dinner is served beneath the loggia,
before the ever-changing spectacle of dusk embracing the valley.

In the "linen bedroom" crumpled sheets blend
with trompe l'oeil pillows painted on the wall itself.
An echo of the artist's pastel picture hanging
in the Suite d'Ardoise, brought here by Nathalie
from her Paris gallery.

A passion for discovery

AGAPÈ
Decoration

Agapè literally means love. And Agapè does conjure up gloriously romantic images. Julie started out in the Scandinavian style of revival, cleaning, scraping, revamping doors and cupboards, tables and mirrors, dressers and chests of drawers.

An ideal homemaker-cum-Cinderella, this young *brocanteuse* has a taste for the tactile and she likes her furniture to flaunt its wear, to glow with a range of patinas from the lightest to the darkest shades. Gazing at a blackened desk scattered with curios, one finds oneself imagining the torments of Baudelaire completing *The Flowers of Evil*: "When the low and heavy sky weighs down like a lid."

And there is no shortage of lids since Julie has a consuming passion for cutlery boxes and silver and ceramic services, in particular for ivory faience soup tureens that are always available, either in her shop here or at one of the sales she organizes every year in a Paris apartment. For three or four days, the space is bedecked with her most recent discoveries and can be visited, and indeed used, like a real house—from the office to the children's bedroom (their portrait hangs on the wall), from the dining room where the table stands ready and laid to the kitchen where tea is on hand accompanied by some *biscuits roses* from Reims.

Lids, once again. Lids for containers of every kind that one accumulates and piles into
heaps over generations, hoping they might one day come in useful. Here there are gems
ready to be discovered by the curious: candy canisters, paint boxes, musical boxes, first aid
kits, letter boxes, card index boxes, cookie tins, shoe boxes, toolboxes, hatboxes. Agapè is
clearly afflicted with this obsessive madness—or aggravating phobia—proposing an original
composition made up of tricolor Bolduc ribbon boxes or English bread tins, or else pyramids of
cotton reel boxes picked up in a textile factory in northern France, which could be recycled as
perfect bottomless toy boxes. A real box of treats!

Normandy
Off the beaten path

BORD DE SCÈNE
Collectibles, decoration

Normandy. Garish light at the highway tollbooth. Overhead signs. The familiar images streaking by on the A13 highway west out of Paris, a road traveled so often, so fast. Slow down, take your time, play hooky. Take the Gaillon exit. Les Andelys, Château Gaillard, Giverny. Fleeting impressions of scenes already experienced. Surprise—an antiques and bric-a-brac store! It's a joy to stumble upon, but almost invisible from the road. Visitors are more likely to come across this small country business on the highways and byways of the blogosphere: its young, smiling owner, Christelle, is an Internet antiquer and bric-a-brac hunter, tracking down, patching up, patinating, and displaying her finds on the Web. Everything is beautifully displayed in Christelle's own home, a traditional *longère* nestling in the heart of a peaceful hamlet, discovered with delight by online buyers who travel here to collect their purchases. And since everything (or almost everything) is for sale, the decor is constantly changing—come again soon!

David and Christelle have reinvented their home as a store and showcase for their stock, incorporating their own living space—the kitchen and the series of bedrooms leading off one another under the eaves. Visitors are inquisitive—is this lamp for sale? You may have to wait for Christelle to unveil her next haul of treasures online, via her blog. There's no hurry!

Elegant

Anjou
The cradle of history

THE CHÂTEAU DE BOISSIMON
Guesthouse

Welcome to the château. Its historical name is "Boissimon," but it's commonly known as "Linières," taking its nickname from the tiny Anjou village where it has always been the center of attention. Although not famous like its fellow châteaus of the Loire—Saumur, Chinon, and Angers—it shares much of their rich past. The Loire River, as is well known, has been far from a tranquil river. The first stones of Boissimon were laid in the thirteenth century, but the Hundred Year's War erased all traces of the castle's far-off medieval past. Nothing remains of the fortified castle it probably once was; what we see today is an elegant Renaissance edifice dressed in limestone and topped with steep roofs of Angers gray slate. Each era and each owner has made a contribution: extending or transforming, and adding further chapters to its history. The last notable event took place in 1949, when Prince Louis Napoléon Bonaparte held his wedding there. After that, for a long time, nothing of import happened, and the château seemed destined to decay. Then, at the turn of the twenty-first century, Chantal and Yves, in an anachronistic fairy tale, fell in love with it and decided to reawaken it.

What was important to them was not so much its showy exterior, but the very essence of the place, an essence they felt impelled to share. And so, like true patrons of the arts, they worked with an interior decorator and a bevy of craftsmen and artists to give the château the finery it deserved. Stripped bare, all the rooms were given a new interpretation, from the floors to the ceilings, the colors to the materials, the furnishings to the smallest decorative objects, mixing Gustavian, Victorian, and contemporary design to create a new non-ostentatious sense of nobility. Of course, Boissimon is luxurious, but its new owners will welcome you with disarming simplicity, and tell you that the true heart of their château is, as in many ordinary homes, the kitchen.

The caravan passes

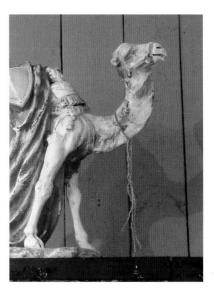

CHRISTINE AND DENIS NOSSEREAU
Antiques and collectibles

L'Isle-sur-la-Sorgue. This dazzling little town in eastern Provence with its daily markets is an essential stopover on any vintage binge. From hangars to storerooms, from Café-Déco to La Petite curieuse, it's a game of leapfrog crossing all the bridges over the Sorgue. At the start of the trail comes the Île aux Brocantes, an urban island and a real treasure trove, while the waltz ends beneath the vine trellis in the Nossereaus' outlet which, without quite knowing why, Christine christened La Caravane passe. It was in all probability because theirs is no fledgling talent, but has been maturing since their earlier forays in the nearby small town of Manosque.

With barely a glance at the trends that come and go, they follow their (own) noses and, with a nicely personal touch, it is their stories, their travels, their encounters that feed into this little oasis, filling it with wooden horses, leaky stuffed bears, cement birds, and other beasts. A crack, a mere scratch, and one is promptly plunged into some distant memory, real or imaginary.

Popular art

The caravan passes, the dogs bark, but popular art endures. Far from art school, these
long-abandoned or long-forgotten objects were handcrafted by anonymous
or marginal artists, and they often betray genuine skill. Carved miniatures or toys, stone
statuettes, scraps of wood and iron, nailed, glued, welded into shape, these untutored
creations—utilitarian or useless—come in all shapes and sizes. Without parallel, this world
is the soul of *brocante*. It finds a perfect haven with Christine and Denis Nossereau, whose
arrangements are works of art in their own right rather than mere displays. The value
of their discoveries lies in their scarcity, in a tremulous beauty each customer perceives
through the lens of his or her individual sensibility and sincerity. And in the final analysis,
it is this that bestows on them such vibrancy.

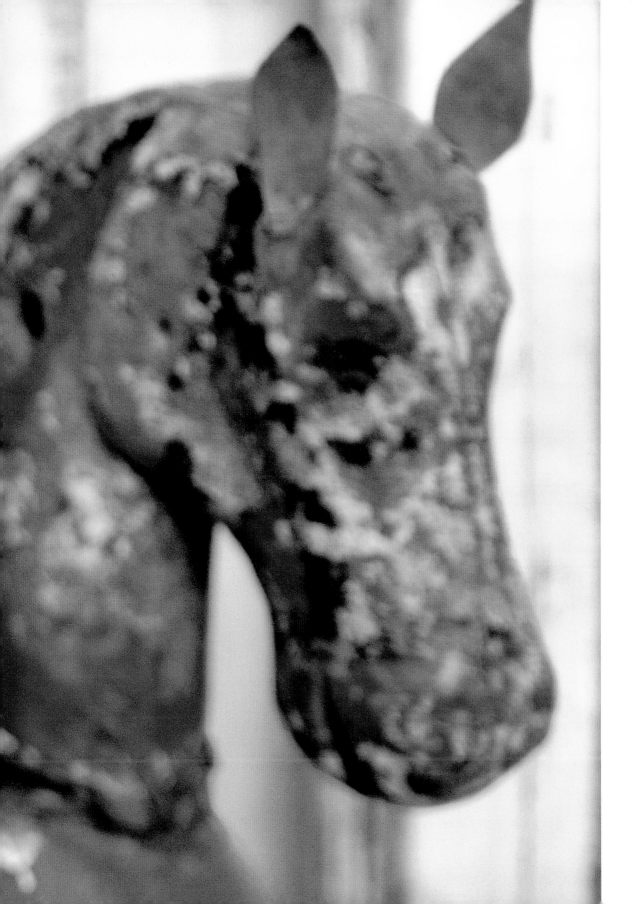

Le Perche
New rustic chic

L'HÔTEL DES TAILLES
Bed-and-breakfast

Saturday morning. The market-day crowds thread the busy streets of Mortagne-au-Perche, resplendent in Barbours and wellies, for a country weekend. Urban visitors do their best to blend in with Le Perche's star village, west of Chartres. French lingerie designer Chantal Thomass has settled here for good. People are admiring the new decor of La Maison Fassier, now privately owned; lingering over lunch at La Vie en Rouge. Away from the beating heart of the village, those in the know meet at their very own *bar des amis*. The red lantern is lit—the Red Bar is open for business! Behind the counter at this informal bistro, Pierre has prepared a platter of cold meats to share, Armelle displays her latest vintage finds. Through the steamed-up windows, we glimpse the facade of their home, the Hôtel des Tailles. The talk is lively, and stories flow with the wine. If only this place could talk, too.

A judicious blend of styles

A fine eighteenth-century residence, the Hôtel Hocquart de Montfermeil was the house of the local tax collector until the fall of the Ancien Régime. A few revolutions later, after many subsequent owners, it is the home of Armelle and Pierre Santarelli, the charming, unaffected hosts of this exceptional place. First, the guest rooms were installed on the upper floors. Next came the Red Bar and a small art gallery, improvised in the mansion's outbuildings. Everything reflects the owners' perfect taste and restraint. Industrial, ethnic, baroque, Provençal? The decor samples every possible style with elegance and spontaneity.

Paneling in the dining room was stripped and left
untreated as a backdrop for panels featuring hunting
scenes, and a collection of small pictures picked up here
and there. Opening off the dining room, a second
salon mixes industrial objects and ethnic art.

Crimson velvet, linen sheets, impeccable white
paint, and distressed wood: materials and colors
blend in the private world of travelers Armelle
and Pierre. They have lived in Provence,
and settled in Le Perche, for the moment.
Tomorrow they may set out for new horizons.

An urban garden

AUX TROIS SINGES
Antiques and collectibles

Between the Seine and the Marais, the "village" of Saint-Paul is a hallowed spot for antique hunting. If dealers are losing ground to new design and art galleries, a row of storefronts is putting up sterling resistance. On one side there's a connoisseur of Thonet furniture (Au Bon usage), on another there's a retro kitchen utensil and stationary fanatic (Au P'tit bonheur la chance), and a bells and whistles emporium (Le Comptoir du chineur).

Aux Trois Singes has set up residence right in the middle of this hodgepodge. Sylvain goes in for smarter wares, decorative for the most part. He sells, as he likes to put it, "useless" things. Just for the pleasure, the sheer futility of it. You just must have it, that thingamajig in the shape of a guy with a potbelly which is supposedly a German cigar cutter, or that candy box nestling in a papier-mâché Senegalese rifleman who looks as though he's stepped out of an ad for Banania chocolate drink. And there are larger items, too, some on the monumental side, such as classic garden statuary and Medici vases in cast iron or stone. Enough to fill the park in one's country home—or else provide imaginative solutions for a balcony or a reception room back in town. After all, Sylvain (a landscape designer in a former life) specializes in what he loves most: garden furniture in the broadest sense.

The art of the garden

Those traditional garden eye-catchers, Medici-style vases, basins, and bowls regularly turn up at Aux Trois singes. In addition to glass cloches and to eminently practical metal watering cans, Sylvain has a fondness for anything rocaille: pot stands, tables, and sculpture, such as the papier-mâché mushrooms that reappear in the shopwindow every fall. Chic at the beginning of the twentieth century, these often unique pieces verge on folk art. Taking his cue from the furniture on offer—cast-iron or scrap-metal tables whose rough-and-ready patina (aka "grunge") he is careful not to remove—Sylvain patiently tends these nature-inspired trinkets, watering the moss that gathers on the hundred-year-old cement every morning. For was it not Voltaire who recommended we "cultivate our garden"?

Paris

A world of its own

MOMENTS & MATIÈRES
Antiques and collectibles

The time when stall holders and ragmen used to set the Saint-Ouen flea market buzzing is long gone. This mecca of all things vintage, in which one can find absolutely everything, is now one of the most popular tourist venues in all of Paris; as many people are on the hunt for the odd and the rare as are taking a Sunday stroll. Among this tangle of markets, Marché Vernaison is the most intriguing. Winding one's way through its alleyways, the Moments & Matières stand comes as a surprise with its majestic and unique pieces, such as a tailor's dummy with a frozen smile, a gaping bull's-eye or a sulky looking papier-mâché rabbit, jostling for position with scrap iron, pieces of rotting wood, and odd bits of armchairs.

The man who composed this characterful little world, Michel, says that he deals in "the filth of the past," in memories of private suffering that make one want to touch, to know more, to be moved.

Heavy if threadbare wall-hangings, broken industrial furnishings, and giant shop signs—at
first the stand of Moments & Matières seems in step with the prevailing zeitgeist, but one only
has to pass over its inviting threshold to find oneself plunged into a more original and personal
ambiance. Visitors are greeted by a plaster bust of Napoleon III. Whetting the appetite,
phonograph horns converted into ceiling lights illuminate an anteroom where yellowing
volumes lie knowingly about. At the very back of the stall, under the gentle glow from
a chandelier garlanded in jute, a skull (*vanitas, vanitatum!*) presides over this wittily reconstituted
Wunderkammer that harbors some choice finds: shells, apothecary bottles, antlers,
bits of pilaster—all or any of which can, in a flash, whisk one off on an improbable
mental journey through time.

A fairytale setting

QUATTROCENTO
Antiques

Nadège and Franck are antiques dealers by profession. Chance naturally plays an important role in their day-to-day lives, like one special morning, which they still remember today. They had just discovered an old engraved portrait of the mayor of Baugé, a small town in Anjou, when they heard of a house for sale in the same town, 200 miles from their home! One visit was enough: they fell in love with the property at first sight. And the sixteenth-century building turned out to be the former home of—the mayor of Baugé! A sign? The couple quickly brought their fairytale world—part Italian Renaissance, part eighteenth century—to this new setting. With its walled garden, punctuated by a watchtower that once formed part of the town ramparts, the house and its outbuildings have undergone four hundred years of change and transformation. Four hundred years? Like Quattrocento, the new name chosen by its present owners. A happy accident.

The couple's deceptively haphazard decorative choices reveal their shared passions: every room overflows with mannequins used in traditional parades, fairground horses, curios, and *objets de maîtrise* (created by craftsmen to demonstrate their skills). A folding screen painted in shades of blue and ocher graces the sitting room. "We live and breathe antiques, down to our forks and spoons!" smiles Franck. Nadège even uses old French recipes and cookbooks in the kitchen. Will their young children follow suit?

For Félix, antiquing trips with his mother are
a crusade to "save teddy bears." And Pauline
invites her friends to play in her pastel-painted
bedroom, home to a vintage Mickey Mouse,
a rocking horse, and a four-poster bed worthy
of "The Princess and the Pea."

From the house to the shop, vintage bric-a-brac
comes and goes, seldom staying put for more
than a few days. What will become of this set
of multicolored Swedish chairs? Franck waits
to see what tomorrow will bring—ever ready to
set a new scene.

Le Perche
Unbridled splendor

LA MAISON D'HORBÉ
Antiques, restaurant, tea room

Still more angels. While hiking through the groves and valleys of the Perche it's impossible not to stop at La Maison d'Horbé, located on the main square of the town of La Perrière. Since lingerie icon Chantal Thomass extolled its wonders on French television the store has become a sensation. Its story stretches back long before that, however, some fifteen years to be precise, when Jean-Noël and Julien deserted Paris and first took on the seventeenth-century ruin which they have now converted to a country brocante.

Concerned by the preservation of the region's heritage, they have renovated the place bit by bit, investing themselves in the history of the village. Julien writes. Jean-Noël hunts for jewelry from Asia or porcelain from China and elsewhere, for silver canteens, secret boxes, chemists' phials, and for all kinds of curios that make digging through the bric-a-brac here such a delight. In 2002, the duo was joined by Laurent and *La* Maison d'Horbé opened a tearoom serving a light but luxury menu including foie gras or scallops, depending on the time of year. The Maison has since developed into a meeting place where one can run into all sorts of people—tourists, locals, and any of the countless Parisians who have made this neck of the woods their home. One chats about life, swaps stories, and then makes off with something to decorate the house—because even if life's other joys can be ephemeral, this isn't!

Carnival of the grandiose

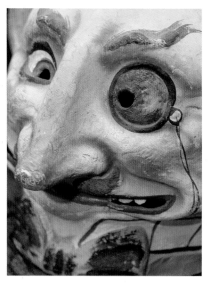

ESPACE NORD-OUEST
Antiques

The first Sunday in September, Lille unpacks its treasures at a gargantuan annual sale that pulls in amateurs and dealers alike, a bantering *brocante* that features everything from cake molds upwards. Aside from this unmissable ritual, vintage lovers might also venture into the byways of a more mysterious Lille. Under the glass roof at Espace Nord-Ouest in Bondues, the dealers' stands almost look like Captain Nemo's cave, where a trio of carnival "grotesques" is not half as scary as the collection of bottles of reptilian creatures pickled in formaldehyde.

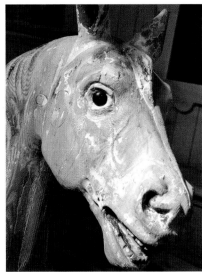

There are no half measures here: "We go for the grandiose." A huge stretch of wainscoting,
a bearskin employed as a door hanging, gigantic metal pigeonhole units studded with rivets,
a larger-than-life wooden horse, and two stone eagles ready to swoop on their prey.
More sensitive souls should make for the welcoming haunt at Marcq-en-Baroeul, Brokidée.
Every room in this onetime Flemish farm offers choice pickings, from the kitchen to the boys'
bedroom via an airing cupboard teeming with trousseaus for the debutante daughters of
the great families of the North. Finish up with a spot of tea or a tasty tart in the hushed decor
of the tearoomat Tous les jours Dimanche… in the heart of Lille's old town.

A distinctive home

LA MAISON MISTRE
Private home

Antiques dealer and interior decorator Franck Delmarcelle has a naturally eclectic, inquisitive mind. Traveling back and forth between his Paris boutique and country retreat, he spotted this curious house in the heart of a Picardy village, for his friend David Mistre. Inspired by the Chinese pavilions greatly in vogue in the eighteenth century, the property stood out proudly from the neighboring brick-clad houses and farms. The weatherboarding and black foundations were reminiscent of seaside properties in the nearby Bay of the Somme—the perfect foil for Franck's decorative touch, his deep respect and passion for traditional techniques and expertise, expressed in his boundless enthusiasm for vintage bric-a-brac, with which he has furnished and decorated the house, from floor to ceiling! Beneath the porch, facing the main gate, a wrought-iron chair from a nineteenth-century garden suite is an invitation to bask in the sun and discover this distinctive guesthouse.

Dinner is served—in the basement! The kitchen is located in the former cellar,

while the garden peeks in at windows opened in the wall, for natural light.

As throughout the house, styles mix and mingle in perfect taste: a Louis XVI

banquette, a rustic farm table, an old grain sack in coarse linen laid as a tablecloth.

On the library walls, mirrors and frames are placed atop the wainscoting of plain, raw planks.
A console supports antique curiosities and a contemporary ceramic vase. A multicolored kilim covers
the floor. The accumulation of styles never strikes a wrong note—including the bedroom, where Empire
style sits perfectly with the quiet charm of the Picardy countryside.

An angelic setting

LA MAISON FASSIER
Antiques

A host of angels. The Fassiers have been cultivating the art of *brocante* for thirty years and their store in the Perche is all about art: an art that borders on the mysterious and the mystical. Still, there's nothing more down-to-earth than the collections they tirelessly amass and offload: sturdy pieces of trade furniture, broad-shouldered workbenches, gears and springs, stuffed animals, and many unlikely curios. But the way their store is arranged transports us to the world of an imaginery science museum, covering everything from the Enlightenment to the industrial era. This off-kilter universe has recently settled into a fitting space—that is, in a grand former girls' boarding school right in the center of Rémalard called, aptly enough, "Ange Gardien" (guardian angel). A moss-covered celestial guardian still watches over the park to the rear of the imposing heap that remarkably, has been converted into a grand house by the couple, who give their "homemaking" talents full rein here. On the ground floor a long corridor embraces kitchen, linen room, workshop, and cabinet of curiosities. Each room fulfills its role, and life transpires in incredible still lifes and compositions.

One is already struck by the carefully stage-managed lighting of the kitchen, accentuated by taxidermed birds, such as the ducks strung up as if after a morning shoot and the hens one can almost still hear cackling. The effect is further strengthened by the sense of touch—by the muscular materials, the rough-and-ready boards, the oily metals and glowing copper, the fragments of stone columns and pediments, the dog-eared books and papers tied up with string, and, finally, the old fabrics and cloths from linen to flax, all given new life by Claudia Fassier. The curios and the workshop are Alain's domain; where he displays a collection of wood and bark in abstract shapes that gives one a sense of the artistic heart of La Maison.

Animals

Together with herbals, seashells, and stones, animals are an essential ingredient in any cabinet of curiosities worthy of its name. Alain Fassier has a penchant for birds, from peacocks to geese; some are shown under glass, others are in the open, hailing visitors to his Maison. As such pieces tend to be associated with hunting and its trophies, they do not always find favor, in spite of their disconcertingly expressive beauty. Nonetheless, a number of them are the fruit of the progress made by taxidermy in the eighteenth and nineteenth centuries, when the aim was to satisfy the thirst for knowledge in natural history among both gentlemen scholars and lovers of the weird and wonderful. Rather than the crocodiles or vanished reptiles, one might prefer a wooden anatomy model, a little carving of a lamb, a stone deer, or butterflies and beetles mounted under glass, which would delight any child who has dreamed of making Noah's Ark as much as it would an entomologist.

Brittany
Granite and hydrangeas

LE MANOIR DE LA VILLENEUVE
Guesthouse

There's no doubt about it; this is Brittany. At the end of the tree-lined drive next to the Villeneuve farm and its hydrangea-trimmed outbuilding stands a lofty manor with imposing granite walls. Their color is not the pink of the seaside town of Perros-Guirec, nor the gray of the Finistère region. Here, the stone hoists the colors of the Côtes d'Armor. The sea, its capes, the seaside resorts of Fréhel, Les Sables-d'Or, Erquy, and Le Val-André, and the distinctively Breton medieval towns of Moncontour and Dinan are a short distance away. Behind the seeming austerity of this eighteenth-century building, Nathalie Pérès has created a comfortable haven that is both calm and romantic. Gray wood trims, blue zinc, parquet flooring, damask fabrics, satin taffetas, chandeliers with pendants, embroidered sheets, and chuckling cherubs decorate the bedrooms, whose old-fashioned names—such as "Rose et Céleste," "Mademoiselle," and "Mignonne"—are an invitation to put time on hold.

Or at least to take the time to make the most of the tender colors of Brittany as found in the paintings of the respected Breton artist Mathurin Méheut, whose canvases hang at the nearby museum of Lamballe. Or to dip into the romantic literature of the coast in the books left at their guests' disposal in the manor's drawing room. Or simply to enjoy the pleasure of a leisurely cup of tea by the fireside.

Flight of fancy

SOUS LES TOITS DE PARIS
Decoration

Born in Paris but "made in Batignolles" (an area in north-west Paris), Gilles calls himself a "creator of environments." And ambiance is one thing Sous les toits de Paris enjoys in abundance. As soon as his first store opened up a stone's throw from the square des Batignolles, he'd sounded a revival in things vintage and started the *brocante* juices flowing. Every lightning visit turned into a conspiratorial discussion over a cup of tea. Times have changed and now Gilles has set up shop right on *the* place to be, but he puts just as much energy into it as before.

A Nespresso machine may have replaced the old teapot, but the fun to be had in this ever-changing little theater remains constant, and the miscellany of objects in the teeming decor is still in a constant state of flux. Two lamps forged from pieces of a Charles X balcony and a pair of riding boots frame the stage. On a black-and-gold enameled tray, glazed plates rub shoulders with a couple of *boules* dressed in tartan. Here, a set of champagne flutes becomes a set of vases for the table; there, the juxtaposition of some specked mirrors and an austere looking stone bust offers food for thought.

Caring neither for style nor period, Gilles makes the most of his stock, be it rare or trivial, functional or functionless—to the point that today his services are sought as an interior decorator. Each new display affords its own batch of surprises and weirdness. New arrivals include a pair of polychrome columns from a seventeenth-century Provençal church that frames a stack of chairs oddly held in place by hoops of rusty scrap metal.

Behind the door, one begins to understand the "cabinet of curiosities" urge that lies behind Gilles's creations. Dried butterflies, a bevy of stuffed deer, volumes with curling pages, all combine into a carefully contrived decor. Sometimes piled onto imposing pieces of furniture (an old counter, an architect's desk, a 1940s glass table), every display takes the form of a mini-museum dedicated to the object—novel, exquisite, intriguing—where a forlorn child's chair can tell the story of a life in the twinkling of an eye.

Still life

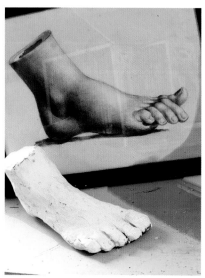

ANGES ET DÉMONS
Antiques

Every angel has a demon. On the banks of the Loire, between the ancient hamlets, the manor houses, and the four-star châteaus, the village of Cunault is noted above all for its Romanesque church. And it is at the foot of this masterpiece that Sophie Prételat has chosen to dwell. She's been into antiques since she was ten and remembers cycling about here as a child netting butterflies. She preserves the passion for freedom that led her to become a *brocanteuse*. Often out and about, inquisitive about everything, her little ark is packed with a wealth of vintage fare.

Every piece of her collection brings a new surprise, with a jumble of unsophisticated and more elevated wares, laid out in lively compositions that invade every nook and cranny of the house. If a puppet that has seen better days shares a shelf with a colorful Santibelli Virgin, a nameless nude with a collection of boxes and wooden flask cases, every one of these objects has a story that Sophie tells with enthusiasm. Often wide-eyed with wonder, as today before a batch of large engravings by Jean-Baptiste Oudry illustrating La Fontaine's *Fables*, she is never above confessing ignorance, reminding us that there is always much to learn, so much so that the demons of this enigmatic and delectable purgatory never fail to lead us into temptation.

Le Perche
Flowers and finds

BOUTIQUE GABRIELLE FEUILLARD
Antiques, florist

A newcomer to the lanes of Bellême, the boutique Gabrielle Feuillard fits in comfortably with the other landmarks of its genre in the region. It is run by Antony Adam, who is both the local florist and a dealer in vintage interiors. Renewed every season, the decor— tended as lovingly as any greenhouse—toys with every style, from baroque to fin de siècle. The diminutive space, structured by a lawyer's filing cabinet or an old shop counter, is then filled with a miscellany of interesting finds: weighty tomes on which time has left its mark, a clutter of candelabras, statues of the Virgin, stoups, crosses, antique frames, even a terra-cotta bust of Molière. Flowers, from old roses to chrysanthemums, naturally grace the backdrop created by this onetime fine art student, who takes his inspiration from the rhythms of the countryside—something his grandmother, the eponymous Gabrielle, taught him.

Until the weather brightens

LE MANOIR DE COUTAINVILLE
Guesthouse, restaurant

Sophie adores the peninsula for its sweeping beaches, the lunar atmosphere of the dunes, and the seascapes and countryside with their ever-changing light and weather. Gazing out over the tousled vegetation of the Cotentin, and across the sea to the Channel Islands, her manor house in the old quarter of Coutainville was the setting for Sophie's childhood family vacations. Today, her warm hospitality is fueled by happy memories of good times with friends and family, and huge, celebratory meals. In the middle of an open field surrounded by high granite walls, the old estate (dating back to the fifteenth century) includes the manor house, a pigeon loft, the seneschal's house, and a barn, all decorated in authentic style, with heirloom furniture, eclectic collections of candlesticks and earthenware, beach games, and wicker baskets. Throw in a trayful of Blainville oysters, Granville shellfish, wild herbs and vegetables fresh from the sandy, salty soil, add a generous dash of good humor from the mistress of the house, and you have the perfect recipe for an island vacation, cut off from the world until the weather lifts.

The manor's outbuildings have been transformed
into a delightful small guesthouse. Next to the fire
stands a wing armchair covered in rich leather
and decked with a tartan throw, complementing
a palette of textiles including finely striped
mattress ticking. The huge kitchen is a delight to
share in all seasons.

Each bedroom is an intimate haven, to (re)discover on your return from
the beach—individually furnished in Gustavian or rococo style, with a mix
of sophisticated and rustic materials (everything from raw concrete to wicker),
and a scattering of chic and ethnic decorative objects. The Sénéchal features
gray-painted walls, bric-a-brac furniture, and a Japanese zinc bathtub facing
the bed—for a touch of manorial Zen.

Along the river

L'HÔTEL DE DIGOINE
Guesthouse

Olivier Dutreil has traveled around quite a lot in Southeast Asia. In fact, his earlier life was centered on the Far East. But he decided to return to France and settle down finally, in the Rhône Valley. Digoine, in the village of Bourg-Saint-Andéol, seemed to have been waiting for him. This vast noble residence, once inhabited by an aging countess, was going to ruin. With Alix, his partner, Olivier undertook the task of getting it going again. He knew that in the past the writers Musset, Stendhal, and George Sand had stayed overnight, and he could have taken these Romantic authors as inspiration for the interiors. Then, in the attic, he discovered the notebooks of a past owner who had been a silk merchant.

This was the revelation Olivier needed for decorative inspiration. The rooms tell the story of the fabled silk roads that led from the banks of the Rhône to China. The homage to the previous owner, in other words, is told in shimmering, colorful silks that also reflect Olivier's past.

Crossing the threshold

CHAMBRE DE SÉJOUR AVEC VUE
Bed-and-breakfast, artist's residence

Here are the keys to the rooms in a guesthouse whose inspiration is in perpetual motion. Head for Saignon, a picture-perfect Lubéron village above Apt. More than just an artist's house, it's a place where art is an integral part of the decor. For over ten years, Kamila Régent and Pierre Jaccaud have been at the helm of this gallery, which also serves as an artist's residence and a guesthouse. The entrance of this lovely Provençal home opens on a line-up of white drapes, an installation entitled *L'Isoloir* (The Voting Booth), which echoes the kind of booth the French use for elections. It's one of several works displayed in the hallways and living spaces.

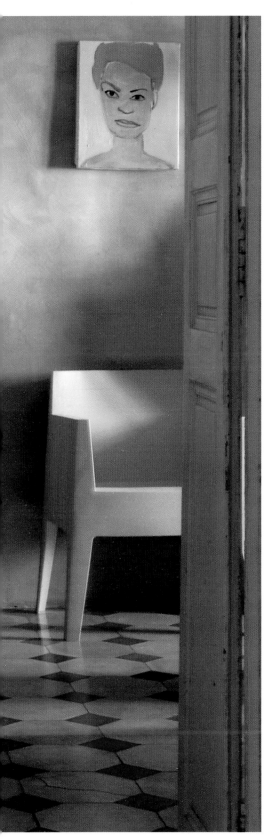

Because this is, indeed, a house where art has its place among the objects used for living. The animal sculpture by Andrzej Wrona, peeping around one corner, will testify to that. In one of the living rooms, a piano that once belonged to the writer André Gide stands side-by-side with an identical bronze miniature. In a hallway, tea is ready on a table but, look, there's a broken cup on the floor.

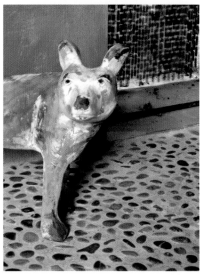

Some hapless guest tries to pick it up, unaware that it is an ephemeral installation. A pair of pajamas hangs in the bathroom. There have been guests who, realizing that they had forgotten theirs, have actually worn these pajamas, only to learn the next day that they belonged to none other than Magritte. This is creativity at its height. It elicits a whole range of reactions and sometimes, even, dubiousness. Can one sit in the garden on one of the Tolix chairs with layers of paint in all the colors of the rainbow flaking off? Is this another work of art? Yes, indeed. These are the chairs on which you will sit for dinner. At Chambre de Séjour avec Vue (Room with a View), welcoming guests has attained a form of high art.

Reveling in whimsy

BORDS D'EAUX
Antiques and collectibles

What people adore about Mers-les-Bains are the madcap rococo villas from the I-do-like-to-be-at-the-seaside years, as well as the cheerfulness of its tag sales, all of which augurs well for finding treasures at the local *brocantes*, from the Alabaster Coast to the bay of the Somme. One might net a batch of wooden decoy ducks at Patrick Deloison's in Saint-Valery (see p. 463), or a mechanical toy such as a "jumping rabbit" or a "pecking chicken"—refugees from the 1980s—at Bords d'eaux. Geoffroy Dassé inherited these entertaining items from his mom, who used to run a novelty beach store. He has lost nothing of his childhood's adventurous imagination, which he exercises daily in his business activities.

And he has a whale of a time, too, jumbling up periods, making the sparks fly, and all because he loves working outside the square, because he chose his profession for the fun, and he never wants it to become a chore. Today, it's a vintage rocking chair designed by Charles Eames that lords it in the middle of the shop, fraternizing with an eighteenth-century table, Napoleon III and Tulip chairs, and a slew of decorative articles ranging from the 1950s to the present day, such as a silicone vase by Italian designer Gaetano Pesce. There's no telling what tomorrow will bring. Though one thing you can bet on is that by then Geoffroy will have repainted the walls and shopfront of his "games room."

The château of a thousand and one lives

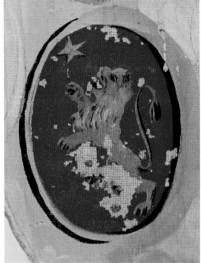

LE CHÂTEAU D'UZER
Guesthouse

The Ardèche is a region of contrasts. Stark stony hills stand out on an arid horizon; the lush gorges for which this part of the world is famous tower above the blue Ardèche River. The road traces out a sinuous line, meandering through the spectacular scenery. Between Alès and Aubenas, it makes its way through the village of Uzer. All is calm; the village appears deserted. Although it may not have the charm of the neighboring towns of Balazu and Labeaume, it is home to one of the most beautiful guesthouses in the region.

And it's a château rather than a house, a genuine château, with a coat of arms, a keep, a guards' room, secret passages, and other surprises—a vaulted ceiling, and a suspended balcony, an exotic garden, and a lovely pool below. Its somewhat deconstructed solidity gives it a timeless quality yet, thanks to the talent, determination, and sheer spunk of the owners, it is also contemporary. And it took an awful lot of all this to get the château back on its feet again. Although Muriel and Éric had urban experience in the renovation business, working in the city was nothing like what they had to undertake in the country. With a tight budget, boundless inventiveness was required: recycling and creativity went hand in hand. The very ordinary Henri II chairs were reupholstered with bright fabrics, transforming the dining room. Stones from the abandoned village train station were laid to edge the swimming pool.

Two caravans were brought to the far end of the garden and converted into stationary accommodations. Against the backdrop of the uneven château stones stands a miscellany of ultra-contemporary objects and pieces of furniture to update the ensemble. While Muriel prepares a generous cuisine of local specialties, Éric hammers away in his workshop at the latest piece of wood or iron he's found to make new garden furniture or another dining table.

Brittany
Full sail

KERELEVEN
Guesthouse

Fine weather, calm seas. A flurry of wind, and Éric Rousseau can sit back and enjoy the majestic spectacle of some of the world's finest racing yachts from his terrace overlooking the celebrated *chenal*—the narrow arm of sea reaching inland from the Atlantic at La Trinité-sur-Mer, in southeastern Brittany. It's a perfect setting. When Éric decided to weigh anchor and devote himself to his first passion—maritime photography—he set a course for La Trinité, one of France's best-known seafaring towns, and a training base for top international yacht crews. Éric spent his vacations here, in a small fisherman's cottage owned by his parents—a traditional *penty* with pitched slate roofs, built in the time-honored way, at right angles to the sea. Extensive work was needed to "turn the house around" and maximize the sea views. Terraces were a priority—and now there are three. Next, the house was extended with the help of local artisans and friends—joiners, carpenters, and painters—each of whom now has a guest room named for him (or her) in the main part of the building. With a nod to the famous Gitana 11 yacht, the winner of the legendary Route du Rhum transatlantic race, Éric has named his house Kereleven: "house no. 11."

Plum-colored walls and headboards made from old doors patinated with gold leaf
and sparse touches of bright yellow or red create a warm, cozy atmosphere in this
bedroom. Éric has brought together contemporary objects and family treasures,
like this antique Hotchkiss trunk, which belonged to the owner's grandfather.

The decor is inspired by cargo ships and sailing
yachts alike. One of Éric's ancestors was
the inventor of the Velox, a nineteenth-century
schooner. To the two-tone walls, extending the line
of the *chenal*'s horizon glimpsed from the window,
animated by the graceful ballet of passing yachts,
are attached old seascapes.

A cabinet of curiosities

SOPHIE AND PATRICK DELOISON
Antiques

There are still people who discover the Somme estuary like Christopher Columbus stepping ashore in the New World. This quiet estuary on the Channel coast of northern France is a fascinating world apart. Patrick Deloison was born here, and played as a child on the narrow streets of the old harbor. Today, with his wife Sophie, he's a mine of information on the finer points of local history, his delight undimmed at the endless ritual of the tides, the shifting light of the bay, its ever-changing moods. Patrick pursues his trade as an antiques dealer with the same passionate interest, collecting decoys of all kinds (ducks, curlews, owls, magpies—the Somme estuary is famous for its birdlife), dioramas, and folk art objects, fueling the evolving displays in the couple's private house and business headquarters, built by Sophie's grandfather in the 1950s. Sophie and Patrick have extended the original building, with a huge two-story wooden verandah overlooking the garden, finished in black weatherboarding, topped with a balcony deck, and lit by two large portholes cut into the side walls, like an elegant liner, ready to sail the seven seas.

The objects and decor in this unusual antique-
dealer's home change as new finds are acquired
or sold, ebbing and flowing with the seasons and
tides. Folk art objects are displayed alongside
tribal sculptures or an exotic, Orientalist terra-cotta
statuette. Like a cabinet of curiosities, amassed
by a seafaring explorer of old.

A long, quiet voyage

LE VAL DE BRANGON
Guesthouse

Partir au hasard. Travel by chance: the phrase invites visitors to explore Le Val de Brangon—Nathalie and Patrick Hubier's guesthouse—online, and in real life. The house is a vast, traditional *longère,* some 120 feet from end to end, nestling between the seaway and lush countryside of the Gulf of Morbihan, in southeastern Brittany. Built in 1824 on the estate of the Château de Kergonano, between the Auray River and the town of Larmor Baden, the former farmhouse was big enough to provide a home for the Hubiers' extensive collections (the couple are dedicated antiquers and travelers). Treasures caught in their net over the years include chunks of ironwork, a ship's porthole, a cargo-ship funnel, wooden doors from India, a propeller, a model plane, stylish furniture, and a host of everyday objects. Scrubbed up, recycled, and put to new uses—practical or purely decorative—everything has found its proper place in the generously proportioned, rambling house that stands waiting to be explored, like a detour on a well-trodden trail of antique shops, skipping from one delightful, unexpected find to the next.

Complementing the *longère*'s original stone
chimney and walls, the owners have added
a touch of bold industrial chic, with untreated
metal fittings and distressed wood—as seen
here in the kitchen, by the design workshop
De bouche à oreille.

Upstairs, the bedrooms lead off a long passageway
under the eaves, each named in honor of Nathalie
and Patrick's passion for their home region,
and faraway places alike. Unsurprisingly,
perhaps, the couple collects vintage
captains' trunks—ready to set sail!

The *longère*'s walls are clad in rusted corrugated iron, coated in traditional red plaster, or stripped back to their original, centuries-old granite. The result is a simple, authentic look mixing rustic, industrial, and sea-port influences.

In the entrance, a cargo-ship's funnel stands like a sculpture against the bare
stone wall, in striking counterpoint to the lush, green landscape to the rear
of the house, overlooking a twelve-acre walnut orchard, beyond which lie
the tranquil waters of the Gulf of Morbihan.

Inspired interiors

GRÉGOIRE COURTIN
Interior designer

They seek him here, they seek him there. Always on the move, Grégoire Courtin plies the town's streets aboard a Segway, and even escapes down the country roads of Navarre, the surrounding region. Courtin is a *brocanteur*, an inquisitive collector, a "home stager," ever on the lookout for rare and unusual objects. His home is his intimate, personal museum. Armillary spheres, terrestrial globes, the accumulated collections of an enlightened amateur. Each carefully placed piece evokes a static journey. But times change: new finds, new projects inspire fresh changes of decor. A life-size saddler's horse, photographed in the living room, has already moved on to pastures new. The decorator always has a storehouse of new ideas up his sleeve. He loves novelty—he moves house often, as the mood takes him—but has never left the shores of the Loire, that bucolic crucible of French history. Renovating, creating color schemes, furnishing, improving: this is what he does best, as an inspired "revealer" of interiors.

A long monastery table, its top painted black—
mounted on casters because it was too low—
stands comfortably alongside an Ikea shelf unit,
its niches decorated with a Roman bust and
a collection of curios.

  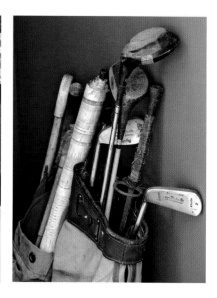

Green pepper, peat, black velvet, incense gray. Dark, muted colors offset the accumulations of objects. A straw boater, fishing baskets, golf clubs, piles of cream earthenware crockery, and—everywhere—books melt into the decor of an outbuilding, which Grégoire lets to guests from time to time. The accommodation offers modern comforts, too—a fitted fireplace and kitchen, and, of course, the serene landscapes of the Tourangelle plain surrounding the village.

Good times and gossip

LES BONS MOMENTS
Antiques and collectibles, tea room

For this journey's end, just follow the signposts to Banon, a village in Haute-Provence, with its delicious eponymous cheese, glorious bookshop, and, not far off, a *brocante*/ tearoom aptly dubbed Les Bons Moments. Ideal for whiling away the "good times" at Banon—such is the philosophy of Marie and Péroline who run this cheerful, laidback venue. As a reward for coming so far, they greet you as if in a roadhouse—but one where tarts and teas from the world over are served to warm the heart, and which contains a gallery proposing writing workshops and temporary exhibits.

BROCANTE

SALON de THE

BROCANTE
SALON de THE
← SUR jardin
"Les bons moments"
GALERIE

As if to repudiate the rarely acknowledged loneliness of a trade they used to practice alone, our two accomplices encourage conversation and introduce people against the constantly changing, indeed "takeout" backdrop that is their store. One used to specialize in period linen, the other in silverware—and now variety is their specialty. A Louis XV *bergère* chair, some dentist's furniture, a little Chinese chest of drawers, a picture showing the parched mountains of their region—they have no preconceived style, because what they revel in most is diversity and storytelling, ideas they sum up in two words: "absolute bliss!"

Chairs

No game of musical chairs here, for at Les Bons Moments there are enough seats to go around. Foldaway garden numbers on the terrace, 1950s lab chairs, or simple school pews under the veranda—forget the traditional Thonets around the table. Metal chairs are the toast of the town at the moment, the most famous being unquestionably the Fermob and Tolix models. Designed primarily for public use, their technical qualities are abundantly clear: they can be set up and stored easily—and they last. Foldable or stackable, various models have long been part of the landscape: the Model A in steel sheet by Tolix, the Bistro model with wooden slats for cafés, or Fermob's Luxembourg in tubing (from the famous Paris garden). How do we know these are classics? The models are still in production today.

Colorful interiors

LA ROSERAIE
Restaurant, guest rooms, vacation
cottage

Barbara and Hans are inveterate travelers. From Canada to Australia and finally here, to a peaceful village in the Morvan national park, a place of lakes and forests, lush meadows and rippling streams. The couple fell in love with the region, and embarked on a new adventure with the purchase of a run-down old inn. Everything "needed doing," but after several months of intensive work, La Roseraie was up and running once again. A small, quiet river, the Ternin, flows peacefully at the bottom of their flower-filled garden—roses, of course. Hans has created a vacation house for guests; Barbara has added a kitchen garden for the seasonal, organic fruit and vegetables, used in her inventive recipes served in the cheerful restaurant—fresh salads and an endless array of tapas. Word of mouth has brought a stream of visitors to enjoy this slice of reinvented life, which opens in the summer months only. Barbara and Hans have other projects lined up: another journey, perhaps another move. A book for sure, which Barbara is currently finishing: *Food for the Soul*, a collection of inspired, heart-warming recipes.

In the library, books and travel guides are cleverly arranged to recreate the colors of the rainbow. Yellow, green, blue, and red—each one a slice of life to savor at leisure. Pages to turn in eager anticipation of the next,unexpected chapter; a tribute to Barbara and Hans's colorful, imaginative approach.

A subtle blend of light and color

Slate, pearl, clay, elephant-hide, taupe, mat white, and lacquered black—La Roseraie is a light-filled setting decorated in soft, neutral shades with bold touches of color, and the yin and yang contrast of black-and-white checkered wallpapers, or plain paintwork. Constantly changing collections of recycled furniture finds, home-made pieces, and clever DIY-deco ideas—including a brilliant system of chandeliers which can be adjusted for height and light—contribute their own style and ambience. The evanescent moods of a simple life, lived day by day, for the moment.

Fridgidaire, Formica, and Meccano

LE VILLAGE POPINCOURT
Antiques and collectibles

Blue-collar Popincourt. Paris *gouaille*—down-at-heel, rough-and-ready, but with a quick wit. Over the last few years, a whole brood of secondhand dealers has set up shop in spots all around the Marché Popincourt market hall. Nobody knows who arrived here first, but today the shopfronts are starting to form a none too orderly line-up worthy of the flea markets of yore. The visit kicks off at La Maison, which beckons us over with its bright turquoise frontage, "Pile-Poil" dog, and the enthusiasm of owner Eléonore, who has lost none of the verve she must have deployed when she worked in "communications." She is, then, an ideal ambassador for the band of artists, craftsmen, and former graphic designers who have been converted to selling antiques. And each does so in his or her own style: Alasinglinglin specializing in stuff from the 1960s to 1980s; Trolls & Puces is fond of trinkets and unlikely recyclings, like a screw-top canister from the legendary Weber Métaux, while its neighbor Belle Lurette is a jack-of-all-trades, selling everything from hollowware to industrial items.

1950s–1970s bazaar

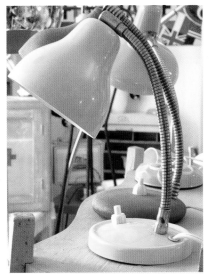  

The 1950s, 1960s, 1970s—the early years of the whole "consumer society" shebang—can be found at Popincourt. And, in particularly good company at Eléonore and Dominique's La Maison, which gives a worthy foretaste of the Ikea generation. Articles both useful and decorative from the booming postwar years jostle for position: metal articulated desk lamps of every imaginable hue, design-style Formica clocks, generic ashtrays and glasses, a cardboard suitcase signed Vespa, an Air Inter cabin bag, an enameled Frigidaire advertising sign, a Polaroid camera.

This gives an idea of the kind of stuff they go in for around here, items snapped up by girls with manga haircuts in transit through Paris, neo-bohemians all misty-eyed about the the "old days" of merciless bartering, or freshly disembarked Parisians on the lookout for something to personalize their tiny apartment, something that'll raise a smile but won't break the bank.

Games and toys

If one wasn't born with the heart and soul of a collector, chasing down old games and toys can still be a real pleasure, not only because they are such obvious fun, but also because inexorably they take you back to your childhood. And some of these toys—whether they be ones we once lost and have forgotten or never even knew existed—are priceless treasures. A pedal car or a rusty tricycle, a clutch of stripy skittles, the frog game (you can still find them in the north of France), a lawn croquet set, a bulk load of Majorettes, some vintage Playmobils, are all more than enough incentive to open one's wallet. And so it is with this Meccano set spotted at Le Marchand d'Oublis (right next to Espace Nord-Ouest) with which one already imagines building an insane mechanical apparatus, some quirky Eiffel Tower or an ocean-going contraption fitted out to dive 20,000 leagues under the sea!

A vintage paradise

UN SOIR D'ÉTÉ
Guesthouse

A May evening. The annual jumble and bric-a-brac sale in the village of Ernolsheim draws to a close. As usual, Nathalie and Frédéric have set out their stall, selling some of their surplus accumulations of objects. They've made some new finds, too—both adore hunting for antiques and vintage pieces. It's a passion, and a way of life, filling their "home museum" with folk art, and twentieth-century decorative and consumer objects: a temple to vintage design. A shrine to sustainability, too, where discarded and forgotten objects are revived and put to new uses, saving them from the bin. And an eminently practical approach, thanks to which the couple have furnished virtually the whole of their Alsatian farmhouse, their home for the past three years. Goodbye to city life! Nathalie and Frédéric are freelancers, young parents, and committed environmentalists. Here, they have found the pace of life they dreamed of. Fred is finishing work on his renovated photography studio, Nathalie runs her advertising agency from home. And their guesthouse brings the rest of the world to their doorstep.

Overlooking the farmyard, the whole house
is open to guests. Half-timbered charm outside,
vintage style within: 1950s sideboards, 1970s
ornaments, even vinyl LPs from the 1980s,
the decor prompts memories of times
not so very long past.

Bertoia, Rietveld: each guest room is a tribute to Nathalie and Fred's favorite pieces, and their designers. They might equally well have been named Jacobsen, Prouvé, Mondrian, *et al*. In addition to vintage pieces of museum quality, the couple collects colorful souvenirs from the heyday of twentieth-century consumerism, the Plastic Years, the years of their teens. Articulated robots and action figures inspired by TV shows of the period, electric wall clocks of all shapes and sizes, rotary dial telephones. Timeless memories.

Nordic spirit

LE MOULIN RENAUDIOTS
Guesthouse

Here is yet another tale of a mill—but nothing outlandish. It's just the simple story of Jan and Peter, who hail from the Netherlands and Denmark. En route for the long journey from their northern countries to the south of France, they made a halt in Burgundy, stopping in the Morvan region where, in Autun, they discovered Renaudiots. It was as if this dilapidated ruin of a mill with its garden run wild had been waiting for them to come along and breathe new life into it. After three years of hard work, the mill was transformed. The interior seemed to have gained space, almost as though the pair had pushed the walls outwards. The now-imposing living room showcases fine, fluted stone columns, highlighted by the workmanlike brushed-concrete flooring.

The combination of country and retro styles (particularly
the 1950s Danish furnishing) creates a mood of tranquillity.
Every detail bears the mark of careful attention: Peter, who
used to work as a designer, has a wonderful collection of
glasswork, displayed like something straight out of a still
life by Giorgio Morandi; Jan, formerly a nurse, grows some
of the produce he serves at dinner in his own garden, *à la
française*. The cuisine, just like the decor, balances elements
of Scandinavian tradition with typical Burgundian dishes:
poached eggs in red-wine sauce, stewed escargots, scallops
with pureed fennel, and free-range chicken with freshwater
crayfish and asparagus. In short, you will find elegant
simplicity in what has been transformed into an enchanting
environment.

Between the sky and the sea

LE SQUARE SEVEN
Bed-and-breakfast

Everyone comes back to Saint-Val. On foot, by bike, on horseback, in the old family Volvo, for a romantic weekend, in hiking boots or barefoot. The Somme estuary and the delightful village harbor are rediscovered each time, like the first. The seasons change, and the setting is as charming and far away-from-it-all as ever. Here are endless skies, the sea, and the birds (everyone comes to the Somme estuary to watch the birds). But there are salt-marsh sheep, too, and an old railway line, a beach shack bar, even a population of seals. Everyone finds their heart's content: the seamen's chapel and cross, the picturesque Courtgain quarter, the Ville Haute. Géraldine has known them all since childhood, and when the opportunity arose to live here all year round— umbrella and Wellington boots at the ready—she didn't think twice. Géraldine settled on a small house in the old medieval town, built of brick, gray stone, and black flint—like the church wall next door. The interior space was remodeled, its walls stripped bare or given a new treatment. Géraldine, a stylist by training, has reinvented the decor, too, in her own subtle, distinctive style.

Lines and volumes are simple, bordering on the
minimalist, like this trompe l'œil wall concealing
a doorway (facing page). Everywhere, there are
fine fabrics and subtle, discreet touches of color:
a bergère covered in crimson velvet, vintage
chairs, a 1950s bentwood armchair chair covered
in natural linen, a group of roses standing tall
in electric-blue glass bottles.

Géraldine has decorated the bedrooms in
a sober, understated but graphic style,
attenuated by pale colors and soft lines inspired
by the ever-changing hues of the broad horizons
of the Somme estuary.

The language of decoration

LES PUCES DU CANAL
Flea market, antiques

It's Sunday morning and Lyon has hardly stirred. But at the flea market Les Puces du Canal, the day is already well under way, as anyone with a passion for antiques will have invaded the well-stocked hangars at dawn. Over the years, the *brocanteurs* have gradually deserted the fancier locations in the city for this weekly get-together at the *puces* market. One's eye is immediately caught by Aisle G and the industrial furnishings and outsized alphabet on Didier's stand. A flea's jump away is Aisle F—that's F for Florence, who shows a flair for trade and industrial furniture, which she combines with creations made of old burlap cushions or mattresses.

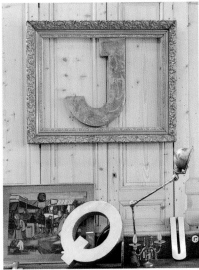

The same clever knack is to be found at Louise's stand a few feet away, and also on Cécile's stand, *Patines* that stocks some wonderful and very collectible trade and shop signs (CHARCUTERIE, or pork butcher; a red TABAC sign in the shape of a carrot).

Trade and workshop furniture

Made-to-measure, unique, imbued with nostalgia for the skills of yesteryear—today, anything with a link to bygone trades and crafts is much sought after. A draper's worktop, a seed rack, a board for clocking-in cards, a set of workshop lockers, and a hardware storage unit still with its stenciled numbers—and the decor is in place. Florence might briefly return a set of wooden shoehorns, some reels of copper wire, some tinplate cookie molds, flasks, and glass bottles, or some mother-of-pearl buttons, to their original use before morphing them into a reception room console table, a rotating photo stand, a business card container, a bookshelf, or even a wardrobe for a child's bedroom. With a glass of white wine in hand, one mulls over one's latest purchases and tries to work out how to get all the stuff home!

Industrial style

ATELIER 154
Antiques, furniture design

The Cité Durmar is one of those retreats that bear witness to the enduring life of the Parisian outskirts. Artisans' workshops and artists' studios dot the verdant cobblestone cul-de-sac. At the very end, Stéphane Quatresous's studio is well attuned to the industrial heartbeat of the area. Wearing a trucker's jacket, a beanie pulled down low over his forehead, this *brocanteur* has, over time, begun to specialize in factory and workplace interiors, becoming a key resource for local architects and interior designers.

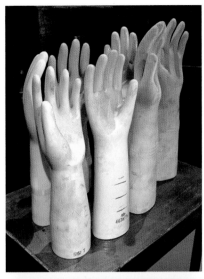

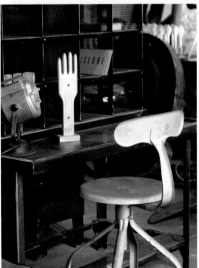

Behind the frosted glass frontage lurks a hodgepodge of the kinds of industrial materials that have the less traditional decorators falling over each other. Whether it be a 1920s mail sorter or some Roneo filing cabinets or crates, Stéphane finds unexpected functions for pieces that prefigured so much of contemporary design, and he has no qualms about mixing them with a brace of Bertoia chairs or an Arne Jacobsen. Here, one can duly appreciate the ergonomics of a Bienaise Studio chair perched on its spidery legs or savor the modular chic of a piece by some anonymous handyman. But there's also the sculptural imagination of a tower of printer's blocks and the ballet-like elegance of a battalion of porcelain balloon molds, featuring coils, rabbits, ducks, and a collection of molded hands reaching skyward, freed from the famous kitchen gloves they used to sport!

Not everyone has the means to acquire a heavy-duty workbench or a set of outsized shelves or tables. In the realm of industrial furniture, lighting is, from a practical point of view, far more accessible. First issued in the 1950s, the Jieldé standard lamp, with its articulated arm and its bulbous reflector equipped with circular handles—making it possible to adjust it without scalding one's fingers—is considered a classic. Rarer are lamps of the Gras style, with a cast-iron base or clamp, which illuminated the worktables of legendary architects such as Le Corbusier and Mallet-Stevens. The less ambitious will easily stumble across workshop or office lamps, telescopic bracket lights that look like insects, or the rows and rows of great enameled iron garage lights with which Atelier 154 abounds.

At the director's house

LE GRAND DUC
Guesthouse

And now we're back in the city, starting off in Valenciennes, in the north of France. Granted, this may not be the spot that immediately springs to mind for a vacation—after all, most people are tempted to go south in search of the sun—but it is here that Philippe Collet decided to place his Grand Duc, meaning "grand duke," the name in French for the Great Horned Owl. As a young diplomat, Collet traveled from his native Lorraine region to Africa. But he put away both his former career and his suitcase in Anzin, where he bought the erstwhile home of a mining-company director. Directly across from the factory entrance, gates open up on a bona fide bourgeois residence, typical of the north of France. A vintage Saab convertible against aged red-brick walls. With a nod to the past, the owner has undertaken refined restoration work, with a serendipitous mixture of modern style, Gothic touches, hints of baroque, and a goodly dose of contemporary art.

Collet is a visual artist, an inveterate antique hunter, a collector of incongruous objects—toy robots, Philippe Starck dwarves, and rubber toads—and ready to talk about his passions, including antique shopping in Belgium and enjoying the northern region he's adopted. Just part of why Le Grand Duc has become the latest must-stay guesthouse near Brussels and Lille.

Carcassonne

A multicolored islet

LA MAISON COSTE
Guesthouse

They were heading south from their native Poitiers and Toulouse, dreaming of Tahiti, but Michel and Emmanuel (better known as Manu), stopped north of the Pyrénées, on the banks of the Canal du Midi. The pair have weighed anchor in Carcassonne, and in the melting pot of this formerly Cathar city they've created their very own colorful island, a reflection of their Robinson-Crusoe ideal. While masses of tourists make their way to the famous upper city, a UNESCO World Heritage site, the Maison Coste remains tranquil down in the lower city.

Already, just a couple years after its opening, it has become a favorite of those in the know. First stop is a look in their boutique for some delightful household object—which invariably leads to a few minutes of rest and conversation in the guesthouse's cozy tearoom. The guestrooms are located on the upper floors, where the colors and design ambience are decidedly Farrow and Ball, the upscale British paint and wallpaper company, and the mood is warm and cheerful. And, for those staying over in Carcassonne or at least spending the evening, there are the dinners and special events like wine tastings that they organize for New Year, Valentine's Day, and other occasions—as well as the garden and the Jacuzzi to which you walk in flip-flops that have been thoughtfully left just for that purpose.

Contemporary

An extraordinary patio

CASA HONORÉ
Guesthouse, decoration

From the secret creeks of the calanques to the cosmopolitan crowds on the city's main thoroughfare, the Canébière, Marseille is France's most exotic mainland city, and the setting for Annick Lestrohan's adopted home: not Brazil, nor a Moroccan *riad,* but a little of each. Behind the imposing façade of the old Roux printworks, on a busy street of workshops above the Old Port, Annick—a professional designer with a string of credits to her name—has created a chic, off-beat townhouse centered on an exceptional patio garden. The industrial building offers some four thousand square feet: enough space for expansive self-expression, whatever its actual size. On the ground floor, a series of interconnecting rooms are the backdrop to an urban lifestyle adapted to the changing seasons: the huge ornamental pond is the focal point of a walkway planted with palm trees, serving an array of salons furnished with deep sofas. Annick has five children already, and now a sixth—Honoré, the name she has chosen for her wide-ranging lifestyle business: a fashion collection, restaurant, and decoration consultancy. Most importantly, though, Casa Honoré is her home.

Honoré includes a collection of fine linens, furniture, and lighting, and an expert
decoration service. The open-work walls resemble traditional *moucharabieh* screens;
original lamps in straw, wicker, or an industrial style set the tone for each room.
Honoré offers a distinctive mix of industrial, Danish, rustic, Moroccan,
and vintage styles and influences: a heady flavor of faraway places.

A château on the coast

CHÂTEAU BORDÉNÉO
Guesthouse

With their ends-of-the-earth quality, as subject to tempests as to sunny skies, the islands along the coast of Brittany harbor reflections of surf and turf that can be rough and austere. And, yet, a lovely château lies hidden on the largest island, Belle Île (Beautiful Island). This château, Bordénéo, is one of the island's most discreet sources of pride. Belle Île—with its wild coast, needle-shaped rocks known as the Aiguilles de Port-Coton and an inspiration to Claude Monet, northernmost Pointe des Poulains, delightful ports of Sauzon and Le Palais, with its Vauban citadel—sums up Brittany and offers a perfect condensed version of its history. The Celts, the Romans, and the Normans all fought for it. The Bretons evangelized it. Later, the British disputed its ownership with the kingdom of France. It was only in the nineteenth century that the situation quieted down, and it became a destination for illustrious tourists, such as Monet and the actress Sarah Bernhardt. The Château de Bordénéo has been a silent witness to all these changes.

In 1870, a Parisian began building a small château in the Italian style, all the rage at the time, on the foundations of a small farm run in the eighteenth century by an Irishman. He gave a very precise brief: a stone house, built over cellars, with a tile roof. There would be a first floor with seven rooms and two bathrooms. Above, there would be four bedrooms for the servants, an attic, and a storage room for fruit. A former mayor of Belle Île has written a well-documented historical account that describes the various owners of the château over the years, who ranged from a charity responsible for saving the shipwrecked to fortunate heirs. The current owners have updated the building, turning what were probably the servants' rooms into stylish bedrooms for their overnight guests. Since they took over Bordénéo four years ago, Françoise and Jean-Luc have made this place and its history their own, while breathing new life into it.

Although lucky enough to have not needed to undertake any major renovations, even discovering intact an astonishing indoor swimming pool in the Oriental style, they have imbued it with their energy and flair. The owners have recently renewed their interior with fine new Loom furniture and chairs to provide a different ambience for future seasons. Perhaps to be joined by the latest works of one of the island's many resident artists.

At home with contemporary art

CHEZ MURIEL LAGNEAU
Private home

Household arts? At Le Canalet, art has taken over the house. Between the limestone plateau of Larzac with its harsh climate and the scrubland of the wine-producing Languedoc region, an imposing turn-of-the-twentieth-century house lies within a quiet green neighborhood in Lodève. Until Le Canalet was established, this small city's artistic fame was more industrially inclined; it was living off its past, when it was famous for the fabric it produced for troops and for its mines. But the construction of the highway and the famous Millau Viaduct, the tallest vehicular bridge in the world and a work of art in itself, was enough to convince a Parisian couple to settle here. Their project was singular: to establish an art gallery that would harbor a few guestrooms as well. After remodeling, the project took hold, offering guests the chance to stay in beautiful natural surroundings within a museum of contemporary art. As soon as you've climbed the steps, you'll find yourself in the thick of things. A hoard of boars—Hausey-Leplat sculptures wrapped in burlap—seems to wander around the entrance.

Your eye will be caught by a mechanical movement: it's a zany automaton designed by Michell and Jean-Pierre Hartmann, the creators of the automated sculptures called "Les Jouets de l'Imaginaire." Each room in the house is an exhibition space. Senegal-inspired furniture from the "Toubab" line, made with recycled metal, and dreamlike paintings by Romain Simon are everywhere to be seen. The trompe l'œil works painted directly onto the walls are the only pieces of art here that are not for sale! Everything else is purchasable, with the sole exception, perhaps, of the top-of-the-line Aga stove that reigns over the guesthouse kitchen.

Flemish elegance

CHÂTEAU LES MERLES
Hotel, restaurant, golf course

White Heather, a thirty-five-meter sailing yacht. And her skipper, Jan van Grinsven. A latterday explorer. One man and his boat—with the family all aboard—traversed the oceans before dropping anchor on the banks of the Dordogne River and falling in love. The object of his desire was a seventeenth-century charterhouse nestled languidly in a hollow of the Périgourdine hills, planted with vineyards. The dreamer's voyage continues, amid the calm reaches of the Domaine des Merles. The *White Heather* is close at hand—in the form of a model, displayed in the gourmet lounge bistro, named in French for its owner's former ship—*La Bruyère blanche*. The estate has its own vineyards and winery, a golf course, spa, and, of course, a hotel. An ambitious program, but unostentatious, on a resolutely human, personal scale. Because life at the domaine is a family affair: Jan's three daughters all live and work here, too.

 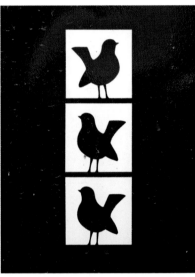 

The decor is the work of the captain's brother, the artist and sculptor Joris van Grinsven. The charterhouse's volumes, atmosphere, and original structure have been subtly underscored with an elegant black-and-white scheme, heightened with eclectic "designer" touches, baroque elements, dashes of color, and a hint of Flemish culture, thanks to reproductions of works by the great Flemish masters.

White walls, black floors. Touches of fuchsia
pink and lime green enliven the restful,
monastic atmosphere.

Isle-sur-la-Sorgue
Starry-eyed

LA MAISON SUR LA SORGUE
Guesthouse

Somewhat removed from the constant hustle and bustle of the antique market for which L'Isle-sur-la-Sorgue is so well-known, at number 6 on the rue Rose Goudard, a door opens on to one of the most elegant guesthouses of the town, an old aristocratic residence with several centuries of history behind it. An enfilade of rooms leads to an immense living room paved in white stone, and this in turn opens on to a courtyard that has been transformed into an oasis of fresh air, complete with pool and an open-air dining and lounging area. The spaciousness of the rooms is enhanced by the skylight that illuminates each floor. Marie-Claire and Frédéric have lovingly restored or kept many of the elements of the past, such as the stone archway and the majestic staircase leading to the bedrooms. They have opted for a minimalist decoration that combines authentic colors and materials, such as terra-cotta and varnished tiles from nearby Apt, with contemporary and ethnic touches. No doubt about it, their love for faraway places sets the tone of their house.

When their guesthouse closes for the season, they take off. Their latest travels have included trips to Vietnam, Indonesia, and South Africa. They return with a bounty of souvenirs, dishes, objects for daily use, cushions, little pieces of furniture, and sculptures like the one they recently sourced in Bali. Their finds are on sale at the boutique just next to the house. Its name, most appropriately, is Retour de voyage (Back from Our Travels), and here they also exhibit the work of selected artists, both friends and those met in distant places, enabling their guests to leave with a tangible memory of their stay.

Bordeaux
Urban rooms

LA MAISON BORD'EAUX
Hotel

Bordeaux, the elegant capital of France's Atlantic coastline, bubbles with excitement these days. Quays have been renovated, and entire neighborhoods transformed into pedestrian-only areas. The town is entering a new era. The Maison Bord'eaux is surfing on the wave of these changes and setting the trend for a new generation of urban guesthouses. Just a few minutes' walk from the heart of the city, this eighteenth-century, former aristocratic residence has a new lease on life, thanks to the initiative of Brigitte Lurton, a member of one of Bordeaux's major wine-producing families.

The owner has introduced an audacious snap of modernity into this classic building, using contemporary materials and vivid colors, and adding touches of 1950s retro style. This is a place to be savored just as much as the wonderful local wines offered at its small private bar.

Cap-Ferret
Hippy-chic

YAMINA LODGE
Bed-and-breakfast

Where in the world are we? In the tropics? On a Pacific beach? No, this is the Atlantic coast, at the tip of Cap Ferret. A fashionable destination as everyone knows; people come to these parts for the soft sand, the pine trees, and the view of the Bassin d'Arcachon. The next best thing to owning a house here is a stay at Yamina Lodge. "Yamina" is the name of the location recorded at the cadastral service. Pascalou has been living in Ferret for twenty years now, dividing her time between her seasonal openings and surfing the best waves of the planet. She's infused her lodge with a style that blends the surfing spirit with hints of Buddhism, adding the hippy-chic style of the Cap Ferret she loves so much.

The lodge is made out of wood, some rooms left unpainted, some painted in the muted tones typical of the area. In addition to an entire villa available for rent by the week (its two bedrooms can be had on a nightly basis except during summer and annual vacation weeks such as Christmas and Easter), there are two completely independent bedrooms. Each has its own look: "La Divine" is immaculate white; "L'Exotica" is multicolored. Natural objects—bamboo sticks, pine trunks, pebbles, and shells from nearby Sailfish Beach—meld into the decor. (The eponymous Le Sailfish is the area's trendy bar to see and be seen in during the summer.) Bicycles are available should you want to take a ride along the quiet streets. Alternatively, you can plunk yourself down on the private west-facing terrace, use the Jacuzzi should you feel so inclined, and enjoy the sunset.

An artist's inspiration

LE PRESSOIR
Country house for rent

Sometimes, a glance at the small ads of a daily newspaper can be the key to a new country life. The advertisement in question—three lines that caught the eye of an urban reader hungry for greenery—announced a "country house for rent, near the market town of Sarlat, sleeps 6–10. Le Pressoir." One telephone call and a trip to the Périgord later, our reader found himself the proud owner of the eponymous "wine press"—a stunning property flanked by a mill race, below the landscaped park of the Château de la Bourlie, officially classified as one of France's *Jardins Remarquables*. A barn, a mill, and three ranges of buildings dating back to the fourteenth century. Cyril de Commarque began restoring the place his way—"barefoot," in touch with nature. An artist, videomaker, and photographer, Cyril has lived in Paris, London, and New York. Now, he's putting down roots and finding inspiration on the upper reaches of the Gironde, the so-called Périgord Pourpre.

Le Pressoir offers spacious volumes, from the living room to the bedrooms. Natural raw materials, vintage Danish furniture, kilims sourced from a souk in Tunis, and pieces made from wood gleaned on the estate. Simple but elegant, the decor inspires a feeling of serenity.

Chalets and seashells

LES GÎTES MARINS
Vacation cottages

The coastal path winds along the broad foreshore, heady with the fragrance of pine trees, privet, and gorse. The walker stops to admire the stunning ancient "rock of marvels"—Mont Saint-Michel—then, catching his breath and continuing on his way, revels in the mingled seascapes and skies of the bay. Olivier Roellinger loves accompanying visitors along the path from his hotel and restaurant at Château Richeux to the Pointe du Grouin. Overlooking the offshore islet known as the Rocher de Cancale, in the grounds of the Roellingers' cottage hotel, Les Rimains, Olivier's wife Jane has installed a collection of family vacation cottages: Berniques, Bigorneau, Crevette, Olivette, and Touline. The delightful "cabins" are surrounded by trees and abundant greenery, each opening onto the gardens and the maritime vegetable plot sloping gently down to the sea. Guests are free to gather herbs and seasonal vegetables here, to cook for themselves, or to dine at the Château Richeux table, where they can enjoy spiced sweetmeats under the watchful eye of the resident chef and his accomplished team.

Children love the cleverly redesigned
berth beds; their parents appreciate
the refined decor.

A fourth house has recently joined
the fleet, architect-designed,
with striking contemporary lines.

A welcoming country home

  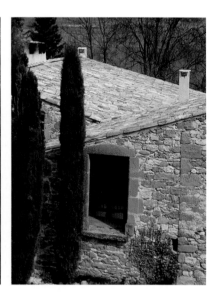

LA BERGERIE DE FÉLINE
Guesthouse

How many city dwellers have dreamed of moving to the country? And how many actually take the step? Brigitte and Jean-Jacques, born and brought up in the southwest of France, are of that rare breed. Before doing so, they embarked on an equally major adventure: a round-the-world catamaran trip with their six children. Once back on terra firma, they set their sights on a more pastoral environment, that of sheep and olive-tree plantations, and weighed anchor in a green valley in the Drôme Provençale region of southeastern France. An old shepherd's barn nestled into a hillside became the focus of their new life on land.

With the help of their families—decorators in the city of Lyon—they remodeled the building entirely, exposing the walls, scraping down the ceiling beams, and sawing blocks of wood. Their tireless efforts have transformed a rudimentary shelter into a welcoming country stopping place, where the authenticity of local materials harmonizes with the design of carefully selected furnishings. Guests who dine here will also get to catch a glimpse of Brigitte and Jean-Jacques's family life: personal black-and-white photos decorate the dining room. You will be able to share their memories of family, travel, and life in the country, while being nourished by the tranquil countryside, images of their children marveling as they witness the birthing of lambs, and the organic bread baked by Joseph, who lives next door.

In full swing

K-ZA
Guesthouse

"K-za" is pronounced in French "ca-sa," as in the word for "house" in Spanish. And this is most definitely the house of Za ... Za being Anne-Elisabeth who, five years ago, left her kitchen in Metz in the east for a piece of Provence. The village of Tulette is located between the so-called Enclave des Papes (Papal Enclave) region and the northern part of the Vaucluse area. It proudly displays its motto: *Toustems libre* (always free). And this suits Za just perfectly,for here she has satisfied her craving for freedom. Her guesthouse was probably a bishop's residence or, more exactly, a residence granted to the bishop during the time—from 1309 to 1377—that nearby Avignon was the seat of the papacy. Avignon today has a major center for theater with an important drama festival, and K-za is having fun at last. Encircled by vineyards, the beautiful bastide is the ultimate in graphic design.

Black metal, rough concrete, and reflecting glass showcase the geometry of the old building. With just a touch of mathematics added in the names of the rooms: 1909, 8½, 3.14116, 69–96, and so on. Some sort of mysterious scientific calculation? No, you won't need your abacus. Not everyone knows exactly how high the Mont Ventoux is, which films Fellini made, what the value of pi is, or about palindromic numbers, but everyone can read between the lines and understand the art of living in this stylish house. Za is talkative, generously doling out her aphorisms, and is especially talented at enjoying life as it comes. She loves to share the hospitality of her land of plenty. Winter is the best season to enjoy the area. From November to March, Za organizes truffle weekends: there's a special menu, local wine auctions and, of course, the Provençal market and hunt for truffles in nearby Richeranches. With her yellow glasses perched on her nose and a green woolen bonnet, Za always sets off with a dried sausage in her right pocket and a piece of cheese in the left, prepared for the evening hour of aperitifs. By the close of the day, her guests also will have come full circle.

Marseille
A rooftop perch

AU VIEUX PANIER
Guesthouse

Marseille, just as you imagined it always would be: its Old Port and narrow, winding streets climbing steeply from the waterfront to the heart of the neighborhood known as the Panier. Between the tall, tightly packed houses, children play, voices echo from behind half-closed shutters, and the sea is a thousand miles away. Looking up, you sense another life, beyond the rooftops. And the view? Just step through Jessica and Pako's front door (a former Corsican grocery store with its picturesque shop front and sign still intact). The young owners—keen travelers, with a strong interest in design and art—have remodeled the interior of this tall, narrow townhouse. After extensive rebuilding, and invitations to local artists to decorate the newly created space, the guesthouse finally opened its doors on the threshold of summer. The terracotta-tiled staircase serves the guest bedrooms, the owners' apartment, and finally the roof—the terrace of their dreams, with a stunning view of the city, its rooftops and balconies, the striped dome of Sainte-Marie-Majeure ("la Major," the much-loved sentinel at the entrance to the Old Port). And the sea—the glorious Côte Bleue—on the horizon.

On the ground floor, the living room and dining room combine to create a friendly communal space. The minimalist black-and-white walls are offset by a decorative mix of vintage, industrial, and Quaker style. One section of wall is covered with a thick sheet of metal, supporting a clever arrangement of magnetized tablet shelves, an ampersand from an old shop sign, and a changing display of posters, papers, and pictures.

Whitelines, Balcon New-Yorkais: each guest room
is named for a different part of the world,
and decorated by a different artist. The Travel
bedroom (previous pages) is decorated with frescoes
by painter Fred Calmets, while Room 3 was designed
by the aKa collective, noted for their work in 3D
(don't forget your glasses!).

Natural

For family getaways

LE SÉNÉCHAL
Hotel, guesthouses

Ten years. A landmark anniversary for Marina and Christophe Ducharme and their small hotel on the Île de Ré, a tiny island connected to the town of La Rochelle since 1988 by the graceful arc of a two-mile bridge. To begin at the beginning: the Ducharmes were married here, and acquired the hotel almost by accident. After experiencing at first hand the difficulties of taking three small children on a hotel vacation, they decided to create their own perfect place for short family breaks. Christophe—a professional architect—took charge of converting the rambling collection of buildings, using every last scrap of space to create a friendly, welcoming home-from-home. With rooms of all sizes and prices, Le Sénéchal quickly attracted an eclectic, enthusiastic clientele. One summer season led to another, bringing new plans and projects. First, extra bedrooms were created in the old Post Office building next door, connected to the hotel by a series of intimate patios and tiny courtyard gardens. Next came a loft, a series of cottages—first one, then two, now four. What will be next?

Beneath a string of firefly lights, the loft typifies the hotel's chic, informal style, with a mix of fine and rustic materials. Old stone, bare brick, and a partition wall of untreated pine along the whole length of the room (concealing the bathroom and WC) create an elegant setting for quality bric-a-brac furniture finds, painted black.

Natural materials and fine patinas

The island's clear Atlantic light suffuses the charming warren of buildings and rooms, connected by their original doorways, partially glass-paned partition walls. Each room is a unique expression of the hotel's distinctive style, and its owners' love of simple, natural materials and objects.

Small stools, church benches, bistro chairs, bamboo garden tables, and a host of other
modest pieces were picked up at bric-a-brac sales in the village, scrubbed bare or
repatinated. Blending perfectly with their setting, each piece embodies the hotel's
essential blend of traditional and contemporary style: unpretentious, simple and full
of charm, like a much-loved vacation home.

Charente
A residence reborn

LE LOGIS DE PUYGATY
Bed-and-breakfast, decoration

A stony road crosses a vineyard. The top of a tower appears, through a gap in the hills. You have arrived at Puygaty. Passing through the entrance lodge, the main residence is discovered at the heart of a complex of fortified buildings. A journey into history. The house is thought to have been used by François I as a summer residence.

Other journeys, other eras: the house's new masters settled in Puygaty six years ago, after a nomadic existence in Belgium and Florida, a taste of the idle life, and vague plans to move to southern Italy. Finally, they dropped anchor in the quiet waters of Charente, on France's central west coast. Their first years here were far from peaceful: work progressed from the main house to the barn. Roofs, doors, and windows needed replacing, walls had to be stripped and limewashed. All the renovation work was carried out using local artisans and techniques, retaining all of the building's great historic charm and character. Pale stonework, whitewashed wood, heavy wrought iron: the building's austere exterior gives little clue to what lies within.

Existing features have been left in their original state. The monumental fifteenth-century fireplace still warms the living room of the main house. Guest rooms have been created in the former stables. Drinking troughs, cribs, and mangers have been incorporated into the plain, understated decor, with a focus on simple raw materials—and essential comforts, of course.

The hosts' refined taste creates a seamless blend of Louis XIII and Venetian styles, with the simple forms of rustic furniture, folk art, and industrial chic. The space and objects recovered in situ have naturally embraced finds sourced from all over the world. As the renovation progressed, woodworkers proved hard to find. Pierre improvised by working with the local blacksmith to create ingenious curtain rails, shelves, steps, and balustrades.

A host of functional or decorative objects in rusted metal fill the house. Pierre and Max have carried on working at the forge, creating their own collection of objects. Their chairs and stools are now available in their boutique and gallery in Puygaty, which also sells signed works by local ceramicists and cutlers. Not forgetting pairs of genuine Charentaise carpet slippers—perfect for visitors seeking rest and relaxation in this quiet place.

Bright ideas

LA SERRE
Antiques, decoration

In the Auge region, a few miles from the sea, we come across this spectacular "greenhouse." Cleared of the waste and of the ivy in which it was once shrouded, it now shelters a curious kitchen garden. Four top-drawer *brocanteurs* concoct strange "pick-and-mixes" that wed the rare with the outlandish: one of them, leader of the gang and head of the academy, is clearly up to speed on twentieth-century interiors, with a collection of riser chairs and comfy leather numbers. Another one strips factories and robs banks—but just for their unique furnishings: hefty filing cabinets, steel pilasters, imposing light fittings, substantial—but empty— Fichet safes.

A third has
unearthed counters
and other oversized
pieces of workshop
paraphernalia,
while the last adds
a romantic touch
with a selection
of painted wood
furniture and
venerable chests
of drawers.

Art and technology

That old dichotomy of art and technology doesn't only provide philosophers with food for thought: it also has pride of place beneath La Serre's glass roof. Craftsmen's equipment, scientific apparatus, elaborate mechanisms of all sorts are liberated from their erstwhile function and exhibited as works of art. Though unsigned, an array of iron sorting tables from the Banque de France seem to bear the stamp of Gustave Eiffel. Meanwhile, a hand-printing press, some lightbulbs, batteries, and a set of factory clocks under glass take flight as ornamental sculptures. An architect's desk complete with rulers, set-squares, and protractors, an optician's apparatus or a copper surveyor's range finder, a Napoleon III cast-iron photographer's stand, or just plans and diagrams for mechanical tools all lead us, of course, into the world of the engineer—but also into the world of the inventor, that artist of the useful and the necessary.

Aude

Child's play

LA MAISON PUJOL
Guesthouse

A, B, C, D. Let's start at the very beginning. La Maison Pujol has a penchant for the letters of the alphabet— made of zinc, wood, or plastic, or painted on canvas—used as simple works of art collected helter-skelter then displayed as if to convey a message. An old neon hotel sign, *AIMER* (love), displayed in capitals on the pebbles of the courtyard, reveals the essence of what Véronique, Philippe, and their children came seeking in this home hidden away in a little village in the wine-growing region of Aude. The thirty-something owners, tired of city life, following the example of a master sommelier, have managed to combine village and family life with running a guesthouse. This has not kept them from continuing their initial careers (one is an architect; the other a designer for a well-known brand).

Their house is open for you to make your own; the children run about, only too happy
to meet new friends. For the Maison Pujol is a playful place, not only for children,
but for adults as well. The minimalist design in the bedrooms balances perfectly with
the easy-going conversation at dinner under the arbor, accompanied by wine from
the Carcassonne area—a natural combination that makes for the good things of life.

As simple as A, B, C.

An open window

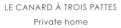

LE CANARD À TROIS PATTES
Private home

Only in the country can you come across a three-legged duck or "*canard à trois pattes*," this one, no ugly duckling, landed in the heart of the Black Périgord region of west-central France— "black," as in the black of the truffles or the black oaks that grow in profusion here—just a short distance from the famous Lascaux Cave, renowned for its prehistoric rock paintings, and the historic town of Sarlat. The origin of this guesthouse's name—chosen by the highly creative brother-and-sister team from Antwerp, Helgi and Greet—remains a secret, but it's plain to see that, with their friend Armand, an artist and painter, they have fashioned something special from the authentic fifteenth-century farm they found in a state of utter ruin in 2000.

Good interior decorators that they are and experts with colors, they reconstructed the building stone by stone, using every single one of the bits and pieces they found on the property, including the increasingly rare, local *pisé* (rammed earth) stones that lay buried by time. When the work was completed with the help of a fourth accomplice, an architect, the main house had been returned to its original state: uneven stone floors, heavy doors, and local-slate roofing.

To replace the outbuildings that were beyond restoring, they put up two cubes of wood and glass. The slim ensemble of buildings fits harmoniously into the surrounding countryside. Echoing the serenity outside, the interior design is markedly sober. Forceful materials—slate, granite, natural stone, and oak, and pure lines of minimalist furniture blend in with the wavy outlines of old beams. The purity is heightened by splashes of color both inside and out: bright paintings, and the blues and greens of the oh-so-bucolic countryside, belying the "black" of the French moniker for the region.

Majestic sobriety

L'HÔTEL D'ALFONCE
Boutique hotel

Make no mistake: Alfonce is not a hotel, but what in France is called a *hôtel particulier*, or an aristocratic town residence—and a very special one at that. The stories that owner Corinne Aubert tells bring added grandeur to the edifice. Built in the seventeenth century, with outstanding features such as a loggia, a spiral staircase, and an imposing Italian Renaissance facade that looks onto a courtyard shielded from the hubbub of the town, the *hôtel* once harbored the escapades of the court of the Prince of Conti. The famed French playwright Molière performed his first plays here for the Contis, at the start of his brief but brilliant career. In homage to the theatrical past of the building and to the notable guests it once hosted,

Corinne, who is also a clothing and costume designer, has given a dramatic feel to her house: polished concrete floors, some high walls plastered with others left in their original state. On one living-room wall you can still see the flakes of former paintwork. The overall sobriety is broken by two tall trompe l'oeil hangings, unearthed at one of the antique shops in Pézenas, that could be straight from a theater set. The two hangings lead to the hallway and the cool, attractive garden. In the midst of this uncluttered decor, the owner has scattered a collection of old glass bottles with porcelain stoppers.

This takes us to the other aspect of Alfonce's history. Jules Aubert, Corinne's ancestor, bought the residence, on credit, in 1883 and set up his lemonade factory inside it. It was only in 1974 that the *hôtel particulier*, now emptied of its soda drinks, reverted to a residence. After major renovations, Corinne has given it a new life with the authentic atmosphere of a family home.

By the white water

LE MOULIN BRÉGEON
Guesthouse

The Industrial Revolution halted work at country mills, and their wheels and blades have long been motionless. The Brégeon mill, built in the nineteenth century, was a sleeping beauty left to go to ruin until the 1970s, when an artist came to awaken it. Jonathan Robinson, an American painter, calls himself an "artistic refugee." Fleeing city life and galleries, he set up his easel within a short distance of Angers and Saumur, between the woods and fields, the châteaus and streams, to pay homage to French culture and heritage. In partnership with two other people, one from Brittany and one from the Périgord, he undertook the renovation of the water mill to transform it into a guesthouse. To the authentic equipment of the mill—cranks, gears, and starting handles—he has added a motley collection of objects from the country and furniture trolled from the flea markets and bric-a-brac stores of the Anjou area.

Lopsided
candleholders,
enameled-iron
hanging lamps,
moss-covered
logs displayed like
sculptures, and sassy
black-and-white
portraits set the tone
for the shabby-chic
feel of the water
mill. But a stay here
is not simply a trip to
the country. For the
three partners offer
thematic tasting
tours in the Saumur
wine-producing area
and French-cooking
lessons using products
purchased at local
markets, picked in the
organic vegetable
garden, or freshly
caught from the river.

These hands-on tours please not only foreign tourists, there to get to know Brégeon and its region, but also all the locals, grateful to the threesome for having created a foundation to preserve the local heritage sites. Even though there is no longer a jolly miller to make bread for the village, the site is just as invaluable today as it was in the past.

Northern France
Setting the scene

LA FERME D'AIGREMONT
Antiques and collectibles, café

I have fond memories of the landscapes of northern France. The forests, pastureland, and rivers of Picardy and the Ardennes, cobbled streets and country roads threading between towns and fields. Here, in the village of Ennevelin, near the Belgian border, I chanced on a small corner of my childhood world—the Domaine d'Aigremont. The *domaine* itself—a fine eighteenth-century manor—has long since disappeared, although its imposing dovecote and drawbridge remain, leading to the home farm, surrounded by the original moat. Behind red brick walls and black-painted doors, Andrée has created a lifestyle that's worth the journey, whether browsing for bric-a-brac (tables patinated with age, faded bergères, lengths of galvanized lambrequin), taking inspiration from Andrée's decorative ideas, or enjoying a bite to eat at the adjoining café. The hands of a huge clock face stand fixed: savor the moment, a tantalizing taste of country living.

The shop sets the tone: restored workshop
lamps, a metal cupboard with its original,
flaking paintwork, an American office chair in
battered leather. Putting old objects to new uses,
browsing, restoring. Create the perfect room
of your own—a place to write, perhaps?
Start a new page, tomorrow perhaps.

Where the mountains meet the sea

LA MAISON DE CONSTANCE
Guesthouse

Constance Ladouceur grew up at Le Château de Sable, her mother's beachside retreat at Cavalaire-sur-Mer. When she decided to create a holiday hideaway of her own, she turned to the last wild stretches of the Côte d'Azur, between Hyères and Saint-Tropez, to the hidden quiet of a region known only to a lucky few. From the extraordinary Mediterranean gardens at Rayol to the secluded village of Ramatuelle, a delightful coast path explores the unspoiled landscapes of the Massif des Maures. Far from the bustling seaside town of Cavalaire, a handful of scattered houses gaze out to sea, and the trio of islands known as the Îles d'Or. Hameau du Dattier is an isolated hamlet, a former stop on the route taken by the historic Train des Pignes. All that remains of the railway today is a long tunnel burrowing deep into the mountain. Constance created her delightful home by connecting two adjacent buildings, surrounded by a swimming pool, and pergolas, terraces, and balconies that were created to make the most of the panoramic views. Far below, Constance can catch a glimpse of her childhood beach, and dreams of other castles, waiting to be built.

The villa is an ideal retreat for large family
gatherings and holidays. The huge living room
and kitchen open onto the terrace, with azure
views of the distant Mediterranean. Constance's
decor draws on her collection of naïf objects
and bric-a-brac finds: a lobster trap, vintage
glass jars filled with dried petals, soft furnishings
in linen and hemp.

Burgundy stone floors and doors made from recycled vintage wood add to the authentic atmosphere and charm of the house. On the upper floor, a large bedroom opens onto a balcony reminiscent of the quirky, hand-built seaside chalets found scattered along this part of the Mediterranean coast. The doors and furniture were all sourced at flea markets, or specially made by Constance's friend Mathilde Labrouche, recreating the raw, naturally worn patina of driftwood washed by the wind and salt water.

New life on the farm

LES GÎTES DE L'ÉTANG DES NOUES
Bed-and-breakfast, vacation cottages

La Grollerie is a five-hundred-year-old farmhouse in the heart of the Mauges, a historic region of rolling hills, valleys, and pastureland near the town of Cholet, south of the Loire—a place even the most determined GPS might be hard pushed to locate. Today, the building is enjoying a new lease on life in the hands of Sophie and Jean-Luc—country children born and bred, teen rebels, and dreamers (Sophie spent time in the northern English city of Leeds, Jean-Luc played in a rock band) and now—following the birth of their daughter, Anna—the proud rebuilders and restorers of this ancient farm, taking them back to their rural roots. Complementing the farm's two gites, the couple have begun keeping animals, just for fun: donkeys, ducks, Angora goats, and Ouessant sheep enjoy the tender loving care of their owners, and their guests' children, who are encouraged to feed, pet, and help look after them. Simple, everyday activities for grown-ups and children to share, on the shores of a small lake, the Étang des Noues.

Maison de coton, maison de lin: Sophie and Jean-Luc have created two guesthouses, available à la carte
for anything from a single night to several weeks. Guests are made to feel completely at home, with attentive
personal touches, cozy rustic comforts, embroidered linen, and farmhouse meals on request. A new approach
to life on the farm: rustic but eminently comfortable, content with simple, shared pleasures.
A utopian dream that has become reality.

Authentic rustic charm

No farm is complete without its farmyard animals:
a crowing cock, fresh eggs, a friendly Mother
Duck (by the name of Josephine) herding her
army of ducklings. Rustic delights, day after day.

A new beginning

LA FERME DES CHAMPEAUX
Tent accomodation

We had read the brochure over and again, noting all the practical details of our planned stay under canvas, deep in the countryside: a blissful country break as promised by the team at Un Lit au Pré, the French arm of the international Feather Down Farm network. We knew what to expect. But arriving at La Ferme des Champeaux was a surprise nonetheless. Owners Amélie and Thomas showed us around our tent: 430 square feet under canvas, with wooden floors, two bedrooms, a cozy boxed-in bed, a wooden worktop, and a wood-burning stove. The children raced down the sloping meadow to play with Viane, Paco, and Luc (who are lucky enough to live here all year round). We didn't see them again until it was time for dinner, eaten by the light of candles and an oil lamp. Nightfall, and the dying embers of the fire. Early next morning, a fine view of the surrounding mountains and the Plateau de Millevaches greeted our amazed citydwellers' eyes. Drinking in the landscape, collecting eggs, fetching milk, walking in the forest, swimming in the lake, collecting wood, lighting the fire. Simple tasks performed every day for a week, yet no two days were the same. And that was all we did: nothing, except share a slice of Thomas and Amélie's lives. Unforgettable moments in an idyllic rural home.

The perfect, picture-postcard country holiday—and memories to last a lifetime. Feather Down Farm vacations were launched in 2003 by Dutch businessman Luite Moraal, a citydweller determined to realize his childhood dream of a cabin in the woods. A dozen prototypes were tried and tested before Feather Down planted its first tent, on a farm in the Netherlands. Each participating farm is chosen with care, reflecting their owners' shared ideals: to help people get back to the soil, and discover the delights of a simpler, greener lifestyle.

Everyday tasks, simple details

Each tent has running water. To heat it, guests light their own wood-burning stove. Newcomers take time
to get accustomed, but quickly establish a routine, learning to take life at a slower, simpler pace. A true luxury!
The luxury of simplicity: the rustic, recycled decor shows attention to detail, and a genuine concern for comfort.
Children fight over the "bed-box" (no camp beds here). There's a big pitcher for fresh milk, enameled tableware,
a kettle, neat rows of egg cups, a traditional larder. The essentials of daily life.

But no electricity! Coffee is ground in an old-fashioned grinder, and supplies can be bought from the grocery store on site (the shower block is installed next door): freshly ground coffee, store-cupboard basics, fresh produce, bread, and pastries all made at the farm. A self-sufficient paradise, far from the madding crowd and its constant race against the clock. Rediscover the joys of living simply, day by day. A new beginning.

An old-fashioned house

CABALUS
Bed-and-breakfast, tea room, gallery

The village of Vézelay, a UNESCO World Heritage site, is perched on the foothills of the Morvan nature reserve. A visit here is a living lesson in history. The village's basilica, a masterpiece of Roman art above the Cure Valley, was once a rallying point for pilgrims, and it's easy to imagine the little town buzzing with excitement as a crowd of the faithful set out for Santiago de Compostela. Hospitality is a long-rooted tradition in Vézelay.

Under the vaults of what once comprised the hostelry and infirmary of the twelfth-century abbey, the couple that own Cabalus house their guests in an atmosphere that seems beyond time. It was a crazy proposal that brought this couple here from Switzerland in 1986, and they became some of the first pioneers in the guesthouse adventure, when they broke with their previous life to take over this spellbinding building. Over the years, they have left their own mark on it with restorations and renovations, all the while respecting the building's rich past and unique ambience. Their special genius? For combining simplicity—of the medieval, monastic type—with the jovial fantasy of their artistic whimsy. With its café-cum-gallery, their house has become a living work of art that defies classification. It's a place you promise to return to even as you are leaving, launching a new cycle of pilgrimage in this little town.

Address Book

When calling France from abroad, telephone numbers begin with the dialing code +33 and the initial 0 is omitted.

Alsace
www.tourisme-alsace.com

UN SOIR D'ÉTÉ page 508
Guesthouse
67120 Ernolsheim-sur-Bruche
06 07 96 90 67
www.unsoir-d-ete.com

Aquitaine
www.tourisme-aquitaine.fr

CHÂTEAU LES MERLES page 578
Hotel, restaurant, golf course
Tuilières 24520 Mouleydier
05 53 63 13 42
www.lesmerles.com

L'ESPRIT DU CAP page 142
Antiques, decoration
2, rue des Pionniers 33950 Cap-Ferret
05 56 60 67 79
www.espritducap.com

LA MAISON DU BASSIN page 164
Hotel, restaurant
5, rue des Pionniers 33950 Lège-Cap-Ferret
05 56 60 60 63
www.lamaisondubassin.com

LA MAISON BORD'EAUX page 588
Hotel
113, rue Albert-Barraud / 33000 Bordeaux
05 56 44 00 45
www.lamaisonbord-eaux.com

MA MAISON DE MER page 246
Bed-and-breakfast
21, avenue du Platin 17420 Saint-Palais-sur-Mer
05 46 23 64 86
www.mamaisondemer.com

LE PASSAGE SAINT-MICHEL page 228
Antiques and collectibles
14, place Canteloup 33800 Bordeaux
05 56 74 01 84
www.aupassage.fr

LE PRESSOIR page 596
Country house for rent
Domaine du Château de La Bourlie 24480 Urval
06 07 10 00 56
www.chateaudelabourlie.com

YAMINA LODGE page 592
Bed-and-breakfast
169, avenue de Bordeaux 33950 Cap-Ferret
06 14 69 36 80
www.yamina-lodge.com

Auvergne
www.auvergne-tourisme.info

LA FONTAINE DE GRÉGOIRE page 10
Guesthouse
Le Bourg 15110 Saint-Urcize
04 71 23 20 02
www.aubrac-chezremise.com

LA GRANDE MAISON, ARTEDU page 26
Bed-and-breakfast, restaurant, workshops
43300 Chanteuges
04 71 74 01 91
www.la-grande-maison.com

Brittany
www.tourismebretagne.com

LA BROCANTE DE JEANNE page 20
Collectibles
Moulin de la Ville Geffroy 22170 Plélo
02 96 74 13 63
www.ferme-auberge-charabancs-bretagne.com

LA BROCANTE D'OUESSANT page 60
Collectibles
Stan Ar Glan 29242 Ouessant
02 98 48 87 87

LE CHÂTEAU DE BORDÉNÉO page 566
Guesthouse
Bordénéo 56360 Le Palais
02 97 31 80 77
www.chateau-bordeneo.fr

UNE CHAMBRE D'HÔTES À DAHOUËT page 253
Bed-and-breakfast
11, chemin du Bignon 22370 Pléneuf-Val-André
02 96 72 88 93
unechambredhotes.canalblog.com

LE CLOS JOSÉPHINE page 285
Guesthouse
8, rue de la Ville Assier 35800 Saint-Briac-sur-Mer
02 99 88 38 42
www.chambre-hote-saint-briac-dinard.com

LES GÎTES MARINS page 605
Vacation cottages
62, rue des Rimains 35260 Cancale
02 99 89 64 76
www.maisons-de-bricourt.com

L'HÔTEL DES DEUX MERS page 133
Hotel
8, avenue Surcouf, Penthièvre-Plage
56510 Saint-Pierre-de-Quiberon
02 97 52 33 75
www.hotel-des-deux-mers.com

KERELEVEN page 452
Guesthouse
11, chemin de la Hune 56470 La Trinité-sur-Mer
02 97 55 75 07
www.kereleven.com

LA LANGOUSTE BLEUE page 90
Collectibles
44, Grande-Rue 35800 Saint-Briac sur Mer
02 99 88 36 98

LA MAISON DES LAMOUR page 116
Bed-and-breakfast, vacation cottages
La Ville Guerfault 22170 Plélo
02 96 79 51 25
www.lamaisondeslamour.com

LE MANOIR DE LA VILLENEUVE page 398
Guesthouse
Saint-Aaron 22400 Lamballe
02 96 50 86 32
www.chambresaumanoir.com

PETITES MAISONS DANS LA PRAIRIE page 176
Bed-and-breakfast, vacation cottages
Le Mourvet noir 22170 Plélo
02 96 79 52 39
www.roselouisemarie.com

LA SEIGNEURIE page 205
Bed-and-breakfast
35114 Saint-Benoît des ondes
02 99 58 62 96
la-seigneurie-des-ondes.net

LE VAL DE BRANGON page 469
Guesthouse
Lieu-dit Brangon 56870 Baden
02 97 57 06 05
www.levaldebrangon.com

Burgundy
www.bourgogne-tourisme.com

CABALUS page 714
Bed-and-breakfast, tea room, gallery
Rue Saint-Pierre 89450 Vézelay
03 86 33 20 66
www.cabalus.com

LA FERME DE MARIE-EUGÉNIE page 146
Guesthouse
225, allée Chardenoux 71500 Bruailles
03 85 74 81 84
www.lafermedemarieeugenie.fr

LE MOULIN RENAUDIOTS page 516
Guesthouse
Chemin du Vieux-Moulin 71400 Autun
03 85 86 97 10
www.moulinrenaudiots.com

LA ROSERAIE page 494
Restaurant, guest rooms, vacation cottage
Le Bourg 71540 Lucenay-l'Évêque
03 85 82 68 95
www.laroseraie.nl

Central France
www.visaloire.com

GRÉGOIRE COURTIN page 478
Interior designer (by appointment only)
06 20 62 67 17

LES PETITES FARIES page 126
Vacation cottage, decoration
28330 Authon-du-Perche
02 37 49 13 69
www.refletsduperche-gite.com

Languedoc-Roussillon
www.sunfrance.com

UN COEUR TRÈS NATURE page 224
Bed-and-breakfast
Place du village 30260 Liouc
04 66 77 43 12
www.uncoeurtresnature.com

LA MAISON page 218
Guesthouse
Place de l'Église30700 Blauzac
04 66 81 25 15
www.chambres-provence.com

LA MAISON COSTE page 552
Guesthouse
40, rue Coste-Rebouhl 11000 Carcassonne
04 68 77 12 15
www.maison-coste.com

LA MAISON PUJOL page 660
Guesthouse
17, rue Frédéric-Mistral
11600 Conques-sur-Orbiel
04 68 26 98 18
www.lamaisonpujol.com

LES SARDINES AUX YEUX BLEUS page 100
Guesthouse
Hameau de Gattigues 30700 Aigaliers
04 66 03 10 04
www.les-sardines.com

Limousin
www.tourismelimousin.com

LA FERME DES CHAMPEAUX page 708
Tent accomodation
87120 Saint-Amand-le-Petit
01 41 31 08 00
www.unlitaupre.com and www.featherdown.com

The Loire Valley
www.enpaysdelaloire.com

ANGES et DÉMONS page 410
Antiques
Rue Jeanne d'Arc 49730 Montsoreau
06 03 56 09 26

LE CHÂTEAU DE BOISSIMON page 322
Guesthouse
49490 Linières-Bouton
02 41 82 30 86
www.chateaudeboissimon.com

LES GÎTES DE L'ÉTANG DES NOUES page 703
Bed-and-breakfast, vacation cottages
La Grollerie, L'Étang des Noues 49300 Cholet
02 41 58 87 53
www.lesgitesdeletangdesnoues.com

LE MOULIN BRÉGEON page 680
Guesthouse
49490 Linières-Bouton
02 41 82 30 54
www.moulinbregeon.com

QUATTROCENTO page 362
Antiques
57, rue Georges Clémenceau
49150 Baugé
09 60 50 56 58
www.antiquites-quattrocento.com

Midi-Pyrénées
www.tourisme-midi-pyrenees.com

LE RELAIS DE ROQUEFEREAU page 296
Bed-and-breakfast, vacation cottages
Roquefereau 47140 Penne-d'Agenais
05 53 41 40 62
www.lerelaisderoquefereau.com

Nord-Pas-de-Calais
www.tourisme-nordpasdecalais.fr/

ESPACE NORD-OUEST page 376
Antiques
644, av. du Général-de-Gaulle 59910 Bondues
03 20 03 38 39
www.nordouestantiquites.com

LA FERME D'AIGREMONT page 686
Antiques and collectibles, café
59710 Ennevelin
03 20 59 12 23
www.bruxellesantiques.com

LE GRAND DUC page 548
Guesthouse
104, avenue de Condé 59300 Valenciennes
03 27 46 40 30
www.legrandduc.fr

LE MARCHAND D'OUBLIS photo page 507
Collectibles
70, rue Jean-Bapiste Lebas 59910 Bondues
03 20 11 25 79
www.doublis.fr

Normandy

www.normandie-tourisme.fr

BORD DE SCÈNE page 314
Collectibles, decoration
Hameau Le Bray 27950 Villez-sous-Bailleul
02 32 52 46 18
bord2scene.canalblog.com

BOUTIQUE GABRIELLE FEUILLARD page 416
Antiques, florist
6, rue Ville-Close 61130 Bellême
02 33 73 53 82

LE CLOS BOURDET page 212
Guesthouse
50, rue Bourdet 14600 Honfleur
02 31 89 49 11
www.leclosbourdet.com

LE DONJON page 270
Antiques and collectibles, vacation cottage
43, rue Paul Besson 14360 Trouville-sur-Mer
06 18 95 51 90

FANETTE W. page 38
Antiques and collectibles
93, rue d'Amiens 76000 Rouen
06 85 01 70 12

L'HÔTEL DES TAILLES page 336
Bed-and-breakfast
61400 Mortagne-au-Perche
02 33 73 69 09
www.hoteldestailles.com

LA MAISON D'HORBÉ page 372
Antiques, restaurant, tea room
Le Bourg 61360 La Perrière
02 33 73 18 41

LA MAISON FASSIER page 390
Antiques
21 rue Ville Close 61130 Bellême
06 07 34 36 72

LE MANOIR DE COUTAINVILLE page 419
Guesthouse, restaurant
2, rue de la Maugerie 50230 Agon-Coutainville
02 33 47 05 90
www.manoir-de-coutainville.com

CHRISTINE AND DENIS NOSSEREAU page 328
Antiques and collectibles (by appointment only)
06 08 82 63 05
www.nossereau.fr

LA SERRE page 654
Antiques, decoration
Route de Cormeilles 14130 Bonneville-la-Louvet
02 31 64 03 21
www.laserredecoration.com

VILLAGE DU VAL D'HUISNE page 72
Antiques and collectibles
RN23 direction Le Mans
28400 Nogent-le-Rotrou
06 86 93 10 15

Paris

AGAPÈ page 306
Decoration (by appointment only)
06 12 57 56 68
www.agapedeco.com

ATELIER 154 page 540
Antiques, furniture design
154, rue Oberkampf 75011 Paris
06 62 32 79 06
www.lateliers.com

L'HEURE BLEUE page 236
Antiques and collectibles
www.heurebleueantiques.com

MAMIE GÂTEAUX page 188
Collectibles, tea room
70, rue du Cherche-Midi 75006 Paris
01 45 44 36 63
www.mamie-gateaux.com

MOMENTS & MATIÈRES page 354
Antiques and collectibles
Puces de Saint-Ouen Marché Vernaison
Allée 1, Stands 13 et 27, 93400 Saint-Ouen
06 77 64 87 12

L'OBJET QUI PARLE... page 86
Collectibles
86, rue des Martyrs 75018 Paris
06 09 67 05 30

SOUS LES TOITS DE PARIS page 404
Decoration
1, place du Docteur-Félix-Lobligeois 75017 Paris
01 46 27 75 49

AUX TROIS SINGES page 348
Antiques and collectibles
10, rue de beaune 75007 Paris
93400 Saint Ouen
01 42 72 73 69
www.aux3singes.com

VERT-DE-GRIS page 292
Antiques (by appointment only)
06 22 86 40 43
www.je-chine-chez-vert-de-gris.blogspot.com

LE VILLAGE POPINCOURT page 502
Antiques and collectibles
3, rue Neuve-Popincourt 75011 Paris
01 48 06 59 47
www.villagepopincourt.com

Picardy

picardietourisme.com

SOPHIE AND PATRICK DELOISON page 463
Antiques
1, quai du Romerel 80230 Saint-Valery-sur-Somme
03 22 26 92 17
www.picardieweb.com/deloison

BORDS D'EAUX page 440
Antiques and collectibles
35, rue Jules-Barni 80350 Mers-les-Bains
02 35 50 12 65

LA BROCANTE DE LA BRUYÈRE page 34
Collectibles
32, rue Campion 60880 Le Meux
03 44 91 12 77
www.brocantedelabruyere.com

LE LOFT page 44
Vacation apartment
(see Sophie and Patrick Deloison)

LE SQUARE SEVEN page 523
Bed-and-breakfast
7, rue de l'Échaux 80230 Saint-Valery-sur-Somme
06 70 90 41 73
www.squareseven.com

Poitou-Charentes

www.poitou-charentes-vacances.com

LE CORPS DE GARDE photo page 725
Guesthouse
1 quai Clémenceau 17410 Saint-Martin-de-Ré
05 46 09 10 50
www.lecorpsdegarde.com

LE LOGIS DE PUYGATY page 645
Bed-and-breakfast, decoration
16250 Chadurie
05 45 21 75 11
www.logisdepuygaty.com

LA MAISON DOUCE page 276
Hotel, tea room
25, rue Mérindot 17410 Saint-Martin-de-Ré
05 46 09 20 20
www.lamaisondouce.com

LES ORANGERIES page 182
Hotel, restaurant
12, avenue du docteur Dupont
86320 Lussac-les-Châteaux
05 49 84 07 07
www.lesorangeries.fr

LE SÉNÉCHAL page 635
Hotel, guesthouses
6, rue Gambetta 17590 Ars-en-Ré
05 46 29 40 42
www.hotel-le-senechal.com

AU TEMPS RETROUVÉ page 194
Guesthouse
30, rue du Havre 17590 Ars-en-Ré
06 82 57 96 09
www.autempsretrouve.com

LA TREILLE MARINE page 158
Collectibles
4, pl. de la République 17410 Saint-Martin-de-Ré
05 46 09 36 22

Provence and the Côte d'Azur

www.provenceweb.fr

LES BONS MOMENTS page 486
Antiques and collectibles, tea room
Place Saint-Just 04150 Banon
04 92 73 39 94

CASA HONORÉ page 560
Guesthouse, decoration
123, rue Sainte 13007 Marseille
04 96 11 01 62
www.casahonore.com

CHAMBRE DE SÉJOUR AVEC VUE page 434
Bed-and-breakfast, artist's residence
Le village 84400 Saignon
04 90 04 85 01
www.chambreavecvue.com

LE CHÂTEAU DE SABLE page 66
Guesthouse
Avenue des Anthémis 83240 Cavalaire-sur-Mer
04 94 00 45 90
www.chateaudesable.net

GRAINE ET FICELLE page 151
Garden produce, cooking classes, guest rooms
and farmhouse meals, ecolodge
670, chemin des collets 06640 Saint-Jeannet
06 85 08 15 64
www.graine-ficelle.com

JUSTIN DE PROVENCE page 170
Guesthouse
Chemin Mercadier 84100 Orange
04 90 69 57 94
www.justin-de-provence.com

LA MAISON DE CONSTANCE page 693
Guesthouse
Hameau du Dattier 83240 Cavalaire-sur-Mer
04 94 00 45 90
www.chateaudesable.net

LA MAISON SUR LA SORGUE page 584
Guesthouse
6, rue Rose-Goudard 84800 L'Isle-sur-la-Sorgue
04 90 20 74 86
www.lamaisonsurlasorgue.com

LE MAS DOU PASTRE page 78
Boutique hotel, gypsy caravans
13810 Eygalières-en-Provence
04 90 95 92 61 80
www.masdupastre.com

LES ROSÉES page 108
Guesthouse
238, chemin de Font-Neuve 06250 Mougins
04 92 92 29 64
www.lesrosees.com

AU VIEUX PANIER page 624
Guesthouse
13, rue du Panier 13002 Marseille
04 91 91 23 72
www.auvieuxpanier.com

Rhône-Alpes

www.rhonealpes-tourisme.fr

LA BERGERIE DE FÉLINE page 614
Guesthouse
Les Charles / 26460 Truinas
04 75 49 12 78
www.labergeriedefeline.com

LE CHÂTEAU D'UZER page 444
Guesthouse
Le village 07110 Uzer
04 75 36 89 21
www.chateau-uzer.com

L'HÔTEL DE DIGOINE page 428
Guesthouse
5, quai Madier-de-Montjou
07700 Bourg-Saint-Andéol
04 75 54 61 07
www.digoine.com

K-ZA page 618
Guesthouse
Route du Moulin 26790 Tulette
04 75 98 34 88
www.maison-hotes-k-za.com

LA MAISON DU MOULIN photo page 732
Guesthouse
Petit Cordy 26230 Grignan
04 75 46 56 94
www.maisondumoulin.com

LES PUCES DU CANAL page 532
Flea market, antiques
1, rue du Canal 69100 Villeurbanne
04 72 04 65 65
www.pucesducanal.com

Index

Acknowledgments

The author would like to thank the owners, designers,
and decorators of the locations explored in
these pages for opening their doors and sharing
their interiors. He also thanks all those who have
encouraged him in the creation of his books.

This book is dedicated to Joseph and Lucien,
and to Laure, loyal and patient passenger of the
adventures in the vintage Volvo, both past and future.

Translated from the French by David Radzinowicz,
Carmella Abramowitz Moreau, and Louise Rogers Lalaurie

Conception and Design: Sébastien Siraudeau

Typesetting: Gravemaker + Scott

Proofreading: Chrisoula Petridis

Color Separation: Altavia, Lille, and IGS, L'isle d'Espagnac, France

Printed in China by Toppan Leefung

Simultaneously published in French as *L'Esprit déco*
© Flammarion, S.A., Paris, 2012

English-language edition
© Flammarion, S.A., Paris, 2012